ACPL ITEM
DISCARDED

MAKING THE MOST OF
ACTION LEARNING

Making the Most of Action Learning

Scott Inglis

Gower

© Scott Inglis 1994

Published by
Gower Publishing Limited
Gower House
Croft Road
Aldershot
Hampshire GU11 3HR
England

Gower
Old Post Road
Brookfield
Vermont 05036
USA

Scott Inglis has asserted his right under the Copyright, Designs and Patents Act 1988 to be identified as the author of this work.

British Library Cataloguing in Publication Data
Inglis, Scott
  Making the Most of Action Learning
  I. Title
  658.40712404
  ISBN 0–566–07452–4

Library of Congress Cataloging-in-Publication Data
Inglis, Scott, 1933-
    Making the most of action learning / Scott Inglis.
      p.   cm.
    ISBN 0–566–07452–4
    1. Executives--Training of.   2. Employee training personnel-
  -Training of.   3. Organizational change--Study and teaching.
  4. Active learning.   I. Title.
  HF5549.6.T7I4573   1994
  658.4'07124--dc20
                                                    94–9706
                                                       CIP

Typeset in 11pt Palatino by Photoprint, Torquay, Devon
Printed and bound in Great Britain by
Hartnolls Limited, Bodmin, Cornwall

Contents

v

List of figures

Preface

Action learning has been with us for over forty years, but the power of action learning has gone unheeded because, being a simple concept, it is difficult to explain.

Action learning can make a decisive contribution to organizational life. The twin concepts of action learning and the learning organization go hand in hand. Today's rapidity of change, whether it be change in the market-place, in customers' foibles, in the social environment or in the way in which organizations structure and restructure themselves, calls for the ability not only to react to change but also to design and manage it. Action learning enables people and organizations to do just this.

This book is aimed at the manager, the chief executive, the personnel director and all those who want to know what action learning can do for their organizations. The discussion of theory is supported by personal experiences and case histories to give a pragmatic approach to implementing action learning.

This book's objective is not only to let managers and others know what they can expect to achieve by investing in action learning, but also to help them to introduce and run an action learning programme.

The first part of the book (Chapters 1–3) provides a general introduction to action learning, describing the underlying theory and principles of action learning, and the benefits which organizations can expect to gain. It sets action learning in the wider context of management training and development and organizational development. The implications of introducing action learning into the organization are also reviewed.

Part 2 (Chapters 4–8) deals with the nuts and bolts of action learning. Starting with the preliminary steps it takes the reader through the all-important preparatory stages and into the start-up workshop – the visible launch of the programme. The preparatory stages and the start-up are described in detail, as is the process of managing the action learning programme during its various stages of development through to the presentation of the results. Chapter 8 looks at aspects of implementing the recommendations made by action learning groups.

Where Part 2 concentrates on the in-company one-project-per-set model of action learning which has been very success-fully used in industry, commerce and the public sector, Part 3 (Chapters 9–11) examines alternative approaches, including the 'classical' open-set model. Between them the one-project-per-set and the open-set, combined with opportunities for joint ventures, allow even the smallest organization to profit from action learning.

Chapter 10 is based on a collection of recent case histories, including some that went wrong and in doing so provided even more learning opportunities. Chapter 11 is devoted to the particular needs of the smaller organization.

Appendix 1 is a series of checklists designed to guide the manager through the mechanics of setting up and running an action learning programme. Appendix II lists a variety of issues which have been addressed by action learning. The purpose of the list to demonstrate the adaptability of action learning and at the same time act as a thought-starter.

The other appendices provide a selected reading list and a list (unhappily short) of useful addresses.

Scott Inglis

Acknowledgements

In my erratic progress through action learning many people have helped and guided me to a better understanding of what action learning is all about. The long list includes colleagues, comrades in adversity, critics and, above all, my clients.

Specifically I should like to thank Richard Bentley, Managing Director of Bentley Woolston, for allowing me to use in Chapter 10 the report which he published following the completion of an action learning programme in his company. Similarly, I should like to thank Sarah Jones for letting me include in the same chapter the article she wrote on the results of a far-reaching action learning programme.

Nor do my close colleagues Dr Barry Lewis of APEC Ltd, and Tony Robinson and Clare Francis of BAB Ltd escape mention: they scrutinized the manuscript and, able to see the wood in spite of the trees, made many valuable suggestions.

SI

Part 1
Background and Benefits

1 The nature of action learning

Action learning is a process which brings people together to find solutions to problems and, in doing so, develops both the individuals and the organization. Alternatively, action learning is a process which develops people and organizations using important issues confronting the organization as a vehicle for doing so.

In action learning these two aspects are always present – the growth and development of people and of the organization, and the simultaneous finding of solutions to problems.

This book has been written for practising managers and for training and development specialists who want to implement action learning and get results. It examines in detail one specific approach, or model. This approach has been well tested in industry, commerce and the public sector. The aim is to focus on the essentials of action learning without over-simplifying, to go back to basics without throwing away the accumulated wisdom of academic research.

The term 'action learning' is a difficulty in itself. Like others who have had to sell the concept of action learning, I struggled hard to think of a title which would be more meaningful to managers. Asked if they know anything about action learning many managers, and quite a few trainers, will say 'yes'. Further questioning will elicit that what they have in mind ranges from action-centred leadership, through action profiling, to outdoor training and even straightforward participative classroom teaching.

Fortunately, I was unable to find a better title. *'Action'* has an appeal to results-oriented managers, and *'learning'* is a constant reminder of what is involved in personal and organizational development.

Today there is an increasing interest in action learning, brought about by the need for organizations to equip themselves for the future by using their own internal resources to address the issues which beset them today. This, and the growing use of action learning in business schools and elsewhere, means that the concepts are becoming much more widely known.

Action learning in action

My introduction to action learning was in the late 1970s. The manager in charge of an oil refinery had asked me to visit him to talk about problems in the maintenance department. The department was not performing well. Steam leaks were on the increase, turn-round times for pumps and compressors were excessive, there had been a spate of equipment failures . . . and so on.

'Can you put together some training for the foremen and supervisors?' was the request.

My answer was that, yes, I could, but I wanted to talk to the foremen and supervisors before I did anything at all.

I spent the rest of that day and the whole of the next closeted with various groups of foremen. They did not like the idea of even more training. They had had all the training they needed. They knew what to do and how to do it. But somehow somebody or something always seemed to foul things up for them – production people, the planners, suppliers, even their own managers.

What they really needed, they explained, was for someone to sort things out so that they could get on with their work.

Courageously, I asked them to confer in groups of half a dozen or so and make lists of the things which were stopping them from doing their job as well as they wanted to.

The initial lists were almost endless, bundling trivial annoyances in with major issues.

Eventually the lists were whittled down until we were left with three significant problems. At this point the foremen were invited to form themselves into three groups (two of five foremen and one of four). Each group was given the task of producing an *implementable* solution to one of the problems.

From the maintenance manager came an assurance that all recommendations would be implemented provided they were feasible, and that he himself would monitor each project to ensure that they were.

'Where do we start? How do projects work? Who can help us?' was the immediate outcry from the foremen.

The answer was to bring in a 'tutor' who had established a reputation for putting across the basics of designing and running a project. He spent two days with the groups. By the end of the second day each group had defined what the problem was and agreed this definition with the maintenance manager. Each group had restated the problem as a project, had calculated what resources they were likely to need, and drawn up a time schedule for completing the project. They were now ready to go.

I had stumbled into my first action learning programme.

Three days later one of the foremen telephoned me. They needed a tutorial on motivation. Having recently been on a 'Motivation in the 1980s' course, I volunteered.

The following week, it was, 'We need to know more about the refinery accounting system.' After three days' strenuous preparation the refinery accountant gave a presentation to the groups and then joined in the project work.

So it went on. Above all else, action learning is learner driven.

Altogether there were eight tutorials during the six-month life of the projects. Five were delivered by tutors from outside the company, the other three by internal specialists.

Other aspects of action learning were clearly in evidence. In their search for information and ideas, maintenance foremen could be seen buttonholing planners, talking to research and development staff, consorting with jetty operators, questioning production engineers, and generally crossing boundaries into different departments. Better still, some went to other companies to see how they had tackled similar problems, and came back full of new insights into their own problems.

Action learning has high visibility. It was clear to all that something different was happening in the refinery. The onus was upon the communication systems to make sure that everyone knew what.

Towards the end of the projects it was suggested that, in addition to submitting recommendations in report form, each group of foremen would give a verbal presentation to the maintenance manager and his 'guests'. The verbal presentations would highlight aspects already covered in the report, and give the audience a chance to ask questions.

The foremen accepted the proposal with some reluctance. In response to their plea for help a presentation skills workshop was laid on. Two years later one foreman confided that after the workshop he had, for the first time, felt confident in preparing and presenting a case to 'management'.

The final outcome was that the recommendations were accepted (with, in one case, some minor modifications) with the foremen themselves deeply involved in the implementation stages.

This case history of a basic in-company programme illustrates several characteristics of action learning.

Action learning is project based   The learning was centred around the need to find solutions to problems. This would make life more bearable for the foremen, hence the appeal to the 'pragmatist' learning style (see below)

Note, however, that while all action learning is project-based learning, not all project-based learning qualifies as action learning.

Action learning is for real   There is an explicit contract between the maintenance manager and the foremen that recommendations will be implemented.

Action learning is learner driven   All the tutorials and the workshop were in response to requests from the participants who also decided when and where to meet and in fact managed their own affairs.

Action learning is a social process   Participants work in groups, learning from each other as well as from tutors and facilitators.

Faced with the difficulties of finding solutions, participants become united in adversity.

Because the social process demands debate, discussion and agreement, the 'reflector' learning style (see below) is encouraged.

Action learning has high visibility   Foremen moved between departments, collecting information and canvassing opinion. They had access to the senior management of the company. It was obvious that something new was being encouraged, that organizational development was taking place.

Action learning takes time   This action learning programme took six months from the first meeting to the final presentation. Most programmes take from four to nine months, excluding implementation.

Action learning: the theory base

There is an essential simplicity underpinning action learning.

Reg Revans, the doyen of action learning, worked from the

hypothesis that even to survive in a constantly changing environment organizations need to adapt – continuously.

Adaptation comes only from learning. Once we have learnt that what worked for us yesterday is no longer applicable today, we start the process of analysing and adapting. But how do we adapt, and to what? The answers can only be found by asking the apposite questions.

A scientist by training, Revans expressed the learning process as

$$L = P + Q$$

where L = Learning
   P = Programmed knowledge
   Q = the ability to pose 'insightful' questions.

Programmed knowledge (P) is stored in books, on tapes, in files. It is accessible – although we may have a long search to unearth it. P dominated our formative school years with facts and figures, dates and formulae. P is the stuff of *Mastermind*, and the purveyors of P are called 'experts'.

P is essential to action learning. Before we move forward in our project work we need to bring our knowledge up to date, and we either call upon the experts (the tutors in our refinery example) to help us, or we engage in desk research. Action learning is often concerned with gaining competitive advantage over our rivals. It follows that a knowledge of the latest techniques and concepts is a vital part of our armoury.

In summary, we pull in the latest appropriate P, and we build on it.

Q, the ability to ask the right questions when everything is uncertain and nobody knows what to do next, is at the heart of action learning. Revans argues that while P is the province of experts, Q is the domain of leaders who want to drive the project forward by getting answers. In this case 'answers' are views, opinions and prognostications.

Q has been described as the political face of action learning. Certainly this is true if, like Bismarck, we define politics as the art of the possible. The results of the action learning programme have to be implemented: anything less may be counterproductive.

Revans suggests that each participant in action learning should have the following questions in the forefront of his or her mind:

1 What am I (or what is my organization) really trying to do, first and last?
2 What is stopping me (or my organization) from doing it?
3 What can I (or my organization) contrive to do about it?

Talking through these questions within the project group (the comrades in adversity) can not only give startling insights into the underlying nature of the problem itself, but can also have a long-term effect upon the way in which individuals approach their work and upon their relationships within the organization.

The first three questions provide a means of tackling the issues underlying the problem. Once these have been answered a second series of questions focuses upon the realities of the situation:

4 Who *knows* about what we are trying to do – who has the *real* facts and can put things into a proper perspective?
5 Who *cares* about getting it implemented – who has a vested interest in getting the problem solved as opposed to merely talking about it?
6 Who *has the power* to get it implemented – who controls the resources that can make change happen?

These are fundamental questions. With its high level of visibility and its insistence upon asking probing, sometimes embarrassing, questions, action learning demands a political awareness and sensitivity from the participants. Action learning requires action to be taken, not merely recommended. Implementation is part of the contract between the company and the project group. Many action learning practitioners would extend Revans's formula to:

$$L = P + Q + I$$

where I = Implementation.

The project in action learning

The project, at the core of every action learning programme, must satisfy several criteria if it is to fulfil its task as a vehicle for learning and an agent for change.

The project must be of genuine significance to the company. This rules out the type of project which is pulled out of a hat to give trainees a 'realistic' problem to work on. The nature of the project will be governed by the level of the participants. I spend a great deal of time working with groups which are made up of senior managers and which occasionally include the chief executive. In these groups strategic long-term issues are the order of the day. With middle management groups tactical or operational issues are more common.

The project must be feasible – it must be within the competence of the group which has been selected to probe the issues and make recommendations. Here we are referring to the collective competence of the group, not to individual competence. Participants will have been chosen for a variety of reasons: some for their expertise in a specific area, some for their ability to produce creative ideas, some for their knack of tying together the fine detail, some because they they need to gain wider experience. The reasons are many, but all have a contribution to make.

If the project is not feasible and falls foul of internecine politics, or if it founders through lack of time, resources or critical skills, the result will be demoralizing for the participants with future action learning proposals being put in jeopardy.

Participants should be challenged and extended without feeling threatened by the prospect of failure, either individually or as a project group. The high level of visibility which an action learning programme attracts means that an ill-chosen project can seriously damage hard-won reputations. In selecting the project it pays to think ahead to the implementation stage – who has the authority to give the go-ahead? Are there likely to be any insurmountable problems?

Fortunately, the action learning process guards us against difficulties such as these. The manager who 'owns' the problem and wants to see it solved is usually the one with the authority to go ahead with the implementation. If not, he knows who to talk to. The thing to check, when setting up the action learning programme, is how committed that manager is to a successful outcome.

The scope of the project is central to the programme. The subject-matter should provide ample opportunity for debate, with many differing opinions being voiced and evaluated. Some time ago I was taken to task by a group of managers for using the word 'ambiguity' to describe a quality I look for in an action learning project proposal. I still believe that this word conveys an essential aspect of action learning: people meeting to develop solutions to a problem, where there is no one answer and the only way forward is to generate and then evaluate a whole range of ideas. It is in the development, presentation and evaluation of these ideas that learning takes place.

The refinery case history concerned maintenance staff carrying out an investigation into maintenance-related problems in their own refinery. They were working on a familiar task in a familiar setting. By definition, most in-company action learning programmes have familiar settings, although, for individual participants, the task itself may be unfamiliar.

There may be distinct advantages in having a project group work in a situation where nobody is familiar with the task. In these situations the insights revealed by skilful questioning can be far-reaching, and the learning opportunities extensive.

Less common as in-company action learning programmes are the unfamiliar–unfamiliar types (box 4 in Fig. 1.1). The nearest we might get could be a group of production managers from several locations going to head office to carry out a project on marketing strategy. Chapter 10 examines these options in more depth.

		Task	
		Familiar	Unfamiliar
Setting	Familiar	1	2
	Unfamiliar	2	4

Figure 1.1   Task and setting in action learning projects

The terminology of action learning

So far we have made an effort to avoid action learning terminology. However, the jargon, once explained, makes for easier understanding and provides a shorthand that all action learning practitioners use. The most common terms, which we shall use from now on, are detailed below.

The set
The group of people, usually five to eight in number, who form the action learning project team. Where numbers are significantly larger, two or more sub-sets may be formed; in the refinery example there were three sub-sets. Individuals are known as set members.

The set adviser
Skilful, knowledgeable and resourceful this is the general factotum who 'services' the set. He or she may be internal (a training and development specialist, a line manager) or external (a consultant or freelance trainer). The set adviser knows the action learning process and steers the set through it.

The set adviser 'facilitates' in the sense of oiling wheels, procuring and briefing tutors, making external contacts, looking after the logistics, and giving moral (and sometimes material) support to the set.

The set adviser is very active during the initial stages of the action learning programme. As the set moves further into the project and members start to take control of their own learning, the set adviser assumes a much lower profile.

The client
The client is the person who owns the problem which is being confronted by the set – in the refinery case, the maintenance manager.

The client has a crucial role to play. Usually a more senior manager, the client's broader perspective can prevent the set going up blind alleys or, for example, moving towards politically unacceptable solutions.

The client's role is critical in ensuring that the set puts forward *implementable* recommendations.

The tutor
An 'expert' who packages and delivers P (programmed knowledge) at a tutorial (witness the refinery accountant and the project management specialist) and encourages Q.

The set meeting
The formal scheduled meetings of the set, normally lasting 3–4 hours. The set meeting may include a tutorial.

Workshops
Normally the only meetings to be held off-site, they may be one-, two- or three-day events where the set can work undisturbed.

Each action learning programme has a start-up workshop (see Chapter 5), and there may be further skills workshops – the refinery presentation skills workshop, for example.

Learning styles and action learning

It is only within the last few decades that psychologists and others have started to explore the way in which adults, living and working in the everyday world, learn. We have to learn just to stand still in the jobs we are doing now. We have to learn continuously merely to keep pace with an ever changing environment.

'How do we learn?' we ask. 'From experience' comes the reply, but for most of us experience is something which happened in the past and from which we may have learnt, although we were not conscious of learning at the time. Learning from experience can be haphazard, full of lost opportunities. As Alan Mumford[1] puts it:

The reality [of managerial life] is that it tends in practice to be hectic, disconnected and highly active rather than reflective, analytical and methodical.

Most learning for most managers most of the time occurs from the process of doing a job; equally, for most managers most of the time, learning is rarely identified beforehand as an opportunity and, only slightly more frequently, identified afterwards as something that happened.

The argument today is that, knowing how we learn from experience, we should be able to become proactive and plan to learn methodically from the experiences we are about to have.

Working in the United States, David Kolb was among the first to develop a theory to explain the nature of experiential learning, identifying four stages in the learning cycle:

1   We start by having a here-and-now experience.
2   We think about that experience, bringing in more data and recollections of previous similar or related experiences – in effect, we mull it over.
3   We continue to think about the experience, but now we are making generalizations and fitting the results into our personal view of reality.
4   We test out our conclusions by using a modified approach the next time a similar set of circumstances arises.

In the UK Kolb's work was further developed by Peter Honey

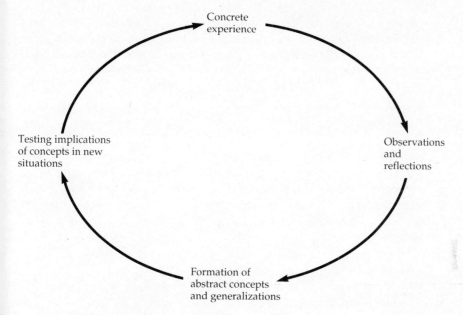

Figure 1.2   Kolb's learning cycle

and Alan Mumford. They recognized that each one of us has four channels through which we learn, although as individuals we prefer some channels to others. These channels are called learning styles, and are named *activist, reflector, theorist* and *pragmatist*. They are listed below, together with a short description of the behaviour associated with each one.[2]

Activists

Enjoy the here and now, dominated by immediate experiences, tend to revel in short-term crisis, firefighting. Tend to thrive on the challenge of new experiences but are relatively bored with implementation and longer-term consolidation. They are the life and soul of the managerial party.

Reflectors

Like to stand back and ponder on experiences and observe them from different perspectives. They collect data and analyse it before coming to any conclusions. They like to consider all possible angles and implications before making a move so they tend to be cautious. They actually enjoy observing other people in action and often take a back seat at meetings.

Theorists

Are keen on basic assumptions, principles, theories, models and systems thinking. They prize rationality and logic. They tend to be detached, analytical and are unhappy with subjective or ambiguous experiences. They like to assemble disparate facts into coherent theories. They like to make things tidy and fit them into rational schemes.

Pragmatists

Positively search out new ideas and take the first opportunity to experiment with applications. The sort of people who return from management courses brimming with new ideas that they want to try out in practice. They respond to problems and opportunities 'as a challenge' (the activists would probably not recognize them as problems and opportunities).

Just as we have our individual preferences in the learning styles we use, most of us have at least one learning style which we neglect. As we shall have a great deal of learning to do throughout the rest of our lives (and that only to tread water) it makes sense to be aware of our own learning style strengths and weaknesses, so that we can plan to learn more enjoyably and effectively. For this reason most action learning practitioners include a session on learning styles in the start-up workshop (Chapter 5).

Having an awareness of his or her own learning styles helps the action learning set member get the most out of the learning opportunities which present themselves during the programme. It also enables the set member to take charge of his or her own learning.

An effectively designed action learning programme allows for the use of all four learning styles, and offers a whole range of opportunities for each style to be practised and developed. Activists will come to the fore when crises have to be dealt with, or visits to other locations made. Reflectors sift through data, examining implications, posing alternatives. Theorists will want to organize all the loose ends into a cohesive framework, asking not a few difficult questions along the way. Pragmatists will be itching to get the new ideas into operation.

What happens if the set takes a deliberate decision to turn this around – giving activists the task of observing and analysing, reflectors the job of dealing with bush fires and other minor emergencies? Theorists can cut their teeth on pragmatism, and pragmatists can work at sharpening their reflector and theorist learning styles.

Closely allied to learning styles is the learning log, which will be discussed in Chapters 4 and 5.

What action learning is not

Action learning is flexible. The approach to action learning described in this book is only one of many, although a very successful one. As well as being flexible, action learning is inventive. Although action learning follows certain well-defined criteria, there is no one textbook methodology.

To the uninitiated action learning can be seen as an *ad hoc* approach, lacking framework and cohesion – despite its emphasis upon working to an agreed schedule, with agreed resources, to achieve a well-defined result. 'Isn't action learning almost the same as . . . ? ', they ask.

Differentiating action learning from apparently similar training, development and management techniques can help us to a better understanding of our subject.

Project work
Projects are part and parcel of organizational life. In any organization, at any point in time, at least one project is under

way. Faced with a problem to which there is no clear answer, senior management will set up a project for more junior managers to grapple with. To that extent, this is also true for action learning – until we look at the composition of the project group. Far from being a mix of learners and developers that we find in action learning, the project group will consist of experts in the subject which *it is believed* lies at the root of the problem. Debate and reflection are often ousted by the need to arrive quickly at the answers; learning is at best incidental.

Where action learning modifies the way in which the organization responds to change, traditional project work, working in ways sanctioned by custom and practice, reinforces the *status quo*.

Project-based management development (PBMD)

All action learning is project based, but not all project-based development is action learning. The criteria for action learning are listed below, and many PBMD programmes meet all the criteria.

Quality circles and total quality management (TQM)

Quality circles have become increasingly popular since the 1970s. After hearing a superficial description of action learning with emphasis upon people getting together to discuss work problems, listeners often ask how action learning differs from quality circles.

Quality circles are part of the total quality management concept, where the objective is to put maximum effort and commitment into completely satisfying the needs of every customer (internal as well as external) in order to acquire repeat business and business by referral.

The essential differences between quality circles and action learning relate to intention and scope. The purpose of quality circles is to react to problems as they occur. The problems themselves are operational, the solutions incremental. In action learning the problems are often strategic, the solutions radical.

Employees certainly develop by taking part in quality circles, but again, this is incidental. Personal development is not seen as a co-equal part of the process.

Business games, case studies and other simulations

'Simulation' is the differentiating factor. By definition, action learning is for real. Those taking part are 'real' people, tackling 'real' problems in 'real' time.

Action learning – a historical perspective

Reg Revans is the name that dominates action learning. Revans himself declares that there is nothing new about action learning. It has indeed always existed, but he was gifted enough to reduce it to a manageable process based on the formula $L = P + Q$.

A Cambridge physicist, Revans started along the road to action learning when he saw how scientists working at the Cavendish Laboratory shared their problems, and received support and help from the others in their group. Later, Revans made a dramatic career change and became Deputy Director of Education for Essex County Council. Then in 1945 he moved from education to industry, becoming the first Director of Education and Training for the newly formed National Coal Board. On arriving, one of his first pronouncements to the NCB staff college was: 'We . . . do not envisage the permanent employment of a staff of qualified tutors, to deliver lectures and seminars.'

This was Reg Revans's first explicit statement about the process which he later came to call action learning.

With the coal industry in public ownership Revans changed the way of doing things: while the staff college tarried, unable to fully grasp the new situation, he went ahead and organized managers into small sets of four or five, meeting in the coalfields, never far away from their own pits.

From the beginning they worked on coalfield problems,

visiting each other's pits and working as consultants to each other (see Chapter 9). These were among the first of many 'comrades in adversity'. Significantly, at a time when most pit productivity remained static, an increase of 30 per cent in output per head was recorded in those pits which took part in the prototype action learning programmes.

By the time Revans had moved to the University of Manchester in 1955 to be the first ever Professor of Industrial Administration in the UK, he had recognized the power of two simple truths:

- members of small work groups learn very quickly from each other
- members of small work groups support each other in achieving output targets.

At Manchester Revans looked for further opportunities to apply his embryonic action learning principles. When he learnt that the Royal Infirmary, which housed the university medical school, was having difficulties retaining trained staff, nurses in particular, he involved those who were seen as part of the problem in solving the problem.

A significant finding was that nurses were discouraged from asking questions and thus from reaching a fuller understanding of their role. This tended to be true of most large hospitals. In contrast, smaller hospitals, where working groups were smaller and communication easier, kept their nursing staff longer.

Success at the Manchester Royal Infirmary led to the Hospital Internal Communication (HIC) Project in London. Small sets of three (usually doctor, nurse and administrator) worked on nearly 40 separate projects over a period of four years. Again, the results were impressive.

Action learning had proved itself at the coalface and in the hospital ward.

The Fondation Industrie–Université of Belgium, a joint venture set up by Belgian businessmen and the country's five leading universities, was the platform for the next stage of development in the application of action learning. Top managers from one industry worked full time in a different industry, looking into problems in areas where they had no expertise of their own. Very much the 'box 4' type of programme in Figure 1.1: unfamiliar task in unfamiliar setting.

In Britain action learning continued to gain converts, although its following was confined to a relatively small number of committed practitioners. Its lack of structure (no 'do this, and this, and everything will be alright'), and the demands it made upon the organization (trust and openness, among others) saved it from a flavour-of-the-month fate.

In 1977 the Action Learning Trust was set up to promote action learning and provide members with a forum for debate. In the early 1980s the Action Learning Trust became the International Foundation for Action Learning (IFAL). IFAL holds conferences and workshops, has an extensive library on action learning, and actively encourages networking between its members.

1982 saw the International Management Centre from Buckingham (IMCB), with Reg Revans as president, start the first MBA programmes based exclusively on action learning. There were two immediate results. Participants on the programmes, the set members, brought about changes within their organizations right from the start of their course. Traditional business schools stood back to see what would happen. Today many business schools use action learning for at least part of their MBA programmes.

IMCB later changed its title to International Management Centres (IMC), with Buckingham remaining the centre for its UK and European operations.

Today the development goes on. Some of the development is in the hands of academics, the rest on the shoulders of training and development practitioners, whether company-based or freelance. One thing is certain: we shall see a dramatic increase in the use of action learning as more and more organizations realize the extent to which it can provide both short- and long-term solutions to many of their problems.

References

1   Mumford, A. (1988), *Journal of Management Development*, vol.
    1, no. 2, Bradford: MCB–University Press.
2   Ibid.

2 The benefits of action learning

Action learning is an investment. Its return can be measured by the extent to which the individual set members grow and develop, by the extent to which the organization becomes more effective in responding to changes in the environment, and by the bottom-line results.

The results are usually measured in the currency of the project, whether this be sales figures, production levels, financial ratios or merely profitability. Not untypical of the results obtained in small companies are those quoted by a chief executive of an organization which embarked upon action learning when faced with the possibility of going out of business:

Gross contribution on sales has risen from a year-to-date average of 32 per cent in October 1990 to 43 per cent in March 1991, and is still on an upward curve. At the same time overheads have been reduced significantly, enabling us to reduce our borrowings by 75 per cent over a five-month period.

These benefits were the result of implementing the set's recommendations. Many of the recommendations were put into effect as they arose during the course of the programme.

The benefits from implementation allowed the company to survive. The benefits which have since enabled it to grow and prosper were the intangible benefits gained from the action learning process itself.

There can be no project – and thus no action learning – without a problem, *even though the problem may be hidden behind a statement*. 'We, the company, do not have a marketing strategy for 1996' is a straightforward statement. But the implication is 'because we do not have a marketing strategy for 1996 we are unable to plan ahead – and will therefore be at a disadvantage in the market-place'. An invaluable benefit of action learning is its ability to focus our minds forward. It gives us a means of preparing for the future as well as coping with the present.

Action learning develops people and organizations

The further we move along the road to discontinuity, the more rewarding action learning becomes.

Over the last two decades the working environment has changed at a rate almost inconceivable in the 1960s. The change has been by evolution rather than revolution and has crept up on us because we have failed to pay any attention to it. Grappling with day-to-day pressures, organizations failed to equip themselves to deal with the ever changing situation.

There was a time when the nature and direction of change was reasonably predictable. The world was much simpler, with less information (we call it 'data' now) to complicate our decisions. There were established ways of doing things, multidisciplinary approaches were the exception, technological change was slower, the market less volatile. All that has now been superseded by an environment in which people and organizations have to adapt continuously to an ever increasing rate of change. The ability to cope with change and manage its implications is now of paramount importance, at both an individual and a corporate level.

Writing in 1987 Tom Peters[1] referred to the all-pervading 'generic uncertainty' brought about by the never-ending introduction of new products with short life spans, by the growth of small, specialist organizations, by the emphasis upon meeting customer demand, however capricious, by the need to cater for and compete in international markets.

In the face of discontinuity, prediction by extrapolation from the past no longer works. How then are organizations to respond?

Action learning provides a substantial answer. Learning, once applied, is synonymous with change. Once action learning is introduced into an organization it immediately sets in motion the process of asking questions, gathering information, and enforcing reflection upon how to bring about change.

Sometimes the questioning may be seen as impertinent, the product of a rebellious child querying the traditions of the elders. (Although we advocate that action learning should be introduced into organizations where a high degree of openness and trust already exist, it is also possible in some instances to use action learning as a vehicle for creating that openness and trust.) Fortunately, most organizations welcome the freedom to question which comes with action learning.

Action learning in effect creates a working context in which people are encouraged to ask, learn and take action in a constantly changing environment where no one person knows exactly what to do next.

Action learning and management development

Management development is about helping individuals prepare themselves for the future by developing their potential. Management development is not *per se* concerned with acquiring new skills or updating old ones – that is the province of training. The distinction between development and training is often blurred, particularly as management development activities frequently include an element of straightforward training.

A benefit of action learning is that it deals with both aspects through the balance of P and Q, using set meetings, tutorials and workshops. In action learning P (the programmed knowledge associated with 'training') serves to provoke Q (the ability to pose apposite questions). Thus it becomes difficult to differentiate between development and training, and in this chapter we use the term 'development' to cover both.

We can, however, distinguish between management development and organization development. The former relates to the development of people as individuals: the latter to changing the way in which organizations corporately respond to the environment. More simply, organization development changes the way the organization behaves.

One of the benefits of action learning is that its high-profile activities within a company send out a very strong signal that the organization is not only open to change, but actively canvassing it. Organization development is seen to be happening.

In Chapter 1 we discussed how personal development can and does take place without our really trying: we grow older, we live through more and more experiences, and we reflect on some of them, but it is all very erratic and half-hearted. Alan Mumford makes the point that managers learn from experience – but badly. What we should be doing is planning to learn from experiences we are going to have.

Action learning provides an immense range of learning opportunities. For many this will be their first experience of being involved in making recommendations which will have a significant effect upon the future of the organization. For many, too, this will be their first taste of management development. For the first time supervisors may be discussing operational and strategic issues with their senior managers. They are being listened to because their views, based on their own first-hand experience, are different and valid.

For some the process of going into other departments to seek out information will be at first intimidating and then enjoyable. Confidence grows, and with it self-esteem.

Many managers still believe that being a manager entails having, and being seen to have, the right answers. Faced with the realities of today's managerial life, and its abundant ambiguities, the result is often stress. This belief in managerial omniscience can break down very rapidly once the manager becomes part of a cohesive set, looking as comrades in adversity into areas where there is no one right answer.

Several managers have told me that the realization that nobody expected them to have all the answers came as a great relief, especially as it was allied with the recognition that colleagues were really there to share problems.

The 'being busy' syndrome is another which disappears in the wake of action learning. In many organizations part of the culture says 'round here managers are paid to be busy and to get things done'. It is comforting, when you have no idea what to do next, to switch on the automatic pilot and engage in familiar no-thinking-required managerial activities. That way you avoid both the pangs of conscience and the necessity of having to think about what to do next.

The ability to work effectively with other people, to influence them and to allow oneself to be influenced by them, is an important outcome of action learning. Two substantial sessions on relationships within teams can be built into the action learning programme. The first forms part of the start-up workshop, the second is a separate workshop run after the set has been working together for several meetings and is beginning to feel the need for more cohesive and effective teamwork.

During the start-up workshop Belbin's Self-Perception Inventory (SPI) (see Chapter 5) is used to illustrate the diversity of managerial tasks, and the extent to which the aptitudes within the group cover these tasks.

The SPI shows how set members have differing preferences – where one member will naturally opt for fulfilling the role of co-ordinator, another may have a natural ability for producing ideas, another for ensuring that the fine details are attended to, and yet another for making sure that everything moves forward according to schedule.

Belbin identifies nine team roles. Ideally all nine should be represented if the team – the set – is to operate at its best.

Fortunately, almost everyone has an affinity for more than one team role, so that even in small sets it is likely that all the roles will be covered, though to differing degrees. If not, the very realization that a team role is missing is usually sufficient for the set to take steps to offset the potential weakness.

This awareness of team roles brings a lasting benefit: participants recognize why other teams and projects they took part in in the past may have failed, or why their relationships with other colleagues were unproductive. The 'practical, no nonsense, let's do it now' individual will be astounded by the realization that there is a dangerous aspect to his natural approach, and may very well start to listen to the previously discounted and underrated colleague whose dictum has always been 'let's examine all the implications and make sure everyone is with us before we go ahead'.

People have started to value their colleagues' perceptions. They now listen to each other.

The team effectiveness workshop reinforces the work done on Belbin's team roles. By the time the set is ready to start the team effectiveness workshop they will have worked together over the start-up workshop and several set meetings. They are now ready to benefit from a more detailed look at how teams work.

To understand what makes one team a high-performing team, another an 'adequate only' team and a third a miserable failure, we need to look again at the attributes which each individual brings to the set. This is not duplicating Belbin, rather it is adding to the individual's self-knowledge and understanding of working relationships from a different perspective.

There is a term 'ERSI'. This stands for 'extraordinarily realistic self-image'. To be able to lead a normal life, communicating with people, relating to them and influencing them, we have to have a realistic self-image. To be a successful manager in today's demanding world, what is needed is a self-image that is *extraordinarily* realistic.

By the time the set has completed the team effectiveness

workshop, they are well down the road towards an ERSI. Each set member will have started the action learning programme with a realistic self-image. This will have been sharpened and brought into each person's awareness. Self-knowledge can now be used proactively, which in turn leads to more effective working relationships and improved personal performance, both in the set and out of it.

The use of instruments such as the Margerison & McCann Team Management Index or the Myers-Briggs Type Indicator during the team effectiveness workshop provides information which has an input into career planning and other human resource management activities – further long-term benefits.

The tutorial inputs which form part of the set meetings provide a rich diet of P (programmed learning). As the set is learner driven the control of P is in their hands, but it is a reasonable bet that among the inputs they request will be:

Managing change: as change is the end-product of the project, the ability to control its implementation is critical.

Creative thinking: sets feel the need to be able to generate ideas. Using techniques such as brainstorming allows them to separate generation from evaluation, with dramatic results.

Project management: having applied the project management techniques learnt during the start-up workshop, most sets call for further help in the middle stages.

Subject-matter specific to the organization will almost certainly be included in the set's shopping list. As in the refinery example, where the refinery accountant gave the tutorial on refinery accounting practices, the tutor will be from within the organization.

Several benefits stem from this: the tutor–manager, in preparing his talk to the brief supplied by the set, has to think through what he or she is going to deliver; in not a few cases this will have triggered change even before the delivery of the tutorial. Secondly, action learning is seen to involve a much wider section of the organization than merely the set members. Thirdly, action learning, by its use of in-house tutors, is seen as belonging to the organization, not to outside consultants.

Making a verbal presentation to the client and his guests (usually the chief executive, the client's own manager, and several colleagues) is a daunting prospect for most sets. Like the refinery foremen, most set members will shy away from what they see (initially a least) as an ordeal. Surprisingly few, even at senior management level, will have had training in making presentations to small groups. Many of those who have had such training will not have practised what they were taught. Sales people, in particular, will have passed, in trainers' jargon, from the state of conscious competence into that of unconscious incompetence.

Running a presentation skills workshop towards the end of an action learning programme concentrates the collective mind and gives a purpose to acquiring the necessary basic skills.

The benefits from this workshop go far beyond the action learning programme itself. The benefits to the individual lie in being able to influence colleagues, customers, subordinates and others by putting a case together and presenting it skilfully and with assurance. Again, self-confidence grows.

Action learning and organization development

A simple definition of organization development (OD) is 'changing the way an organization behaves'.

OD is an inescapable result of action learning: it is not possible to run an in-company action learning programme without its being seen and commented on. People see that fresh methods are being tried. Where action learning is being introduced into a company for the first time, this in itself is a declaration of OD, a public announcement that the organization has embarked upon a new approach to confronting issues and tackling problems.

By using action learning the organization is stating its belief in the ability of its employees to find solutions to critical problems without recourse to external consultants or experts. It is also demonstrating that its senior management is prepared to go out on a limb and admit that it might not have all the answers.

The way in which action learning treats problem-solving is radically different from the traditional methods, where experts apply detailed analysis and various weighting factors to whittle down the possible courses of action until only one is left. Instead of closing down the options, action learning works hard to open them up, increasing the number of possible solutions by involving non-experts whose lack of conditioning to the technicalities of the problem allows them to ask idiot questions – expertly.

Morgan and Ramirez[2] make the point that while many decision-making procedures set out to reduce the variety of solutions by a process of systematic elimination, action learning works at increasing the number of options, encompassing as much variety as possible. The set member with no specialist knowledge may have only a superficial grasp of the problem to begin with. Nevertheless, his or her contribution may be crucial to the success of the project, simply because he or she, as a non-expert, can bring intelligent ignorance to bear, isolating the fundamentals of the problem and at the same time opening up new avenues for exploration.

When an organization adopts an action learning programme it also commits itself to OD. Successful action learning will change the way that managers think and behave, both individually and collectively. This in turn will alter the way in which the organization musters its resources to respond to internal and external changes, the opportunities and the threats. The organizational paradigm will be challenged, and the culture will be modified.

Action learning and self-reliance

A feature of action learning which many organizations see as a benefit is that it can be brought inside the company and operated with a minimum of outside help.

Action learning is bad news for the consultant who wants a client for life. By the same token it is excellent news for the organization that wants to be self-reliant and to have a powerful problem-solving tool constantly at its disposal.

Action learning is a process which has a defined though flexible framework. To work successfully it should be guided into the organization by a specialist who knows both theory and process and has had experience of leading action learning sets in a variety of situations.

A consultant coming into an organization will normally expect to be involved in discussions about the issues to be addressed and the composition of the set. His or her advice may well be sought on the selection and role of the client, but very often no mention is made of a 'shadow' set adviser or a set adviser elect who will understudy the consultant set adviser, not only helping with the logistics of the programme but also preparing to be the set adviser of the future.

Consultant set advisers can easily become embedded in the fabric of an organization. If the organization wants to become self-reliant it must use the initial action learning programme as an opportunity to develop its own internal action learning specialist, the shadow set adviser.

During the first action learning programme the shadow set adviser is first and foremost a set member – what better way to learn what it feels like to take part in action learning? Outside the programme he or she will be spending some considerable time discussing action learning principles and practice with the consultant set adviser. The exact details of the shadow set adviser's role will have been agreed before the start of the programme,and explained to the set and to the client during the start-up workshop.

Having been launched into action learning on the first programme, the shadow set adviser can make use of the intervening period before the next programme to prepare for a fuller role. He or she may be lucky enough to gain exposure to other action learning activities, either through a personal network or through the services of the consultant set adviser. Going to seminars on action learning or attending courses to update appropriate skills is time well spent. Certainly there will be a significant amount of reading to do. Drawing up a list of colleagues and others, internal and external, who can be called upon to deliver tutorials in a range of subjects will expose the gaps in the set adviser's personal network and save time later on.

Although there are a few courses and seminars on various aspects of action learning, there is no single course which deals comprehensively with running an in-house action learning programme of the type we are discussing. However, it is worth checking with IFAL from time to time to see if one does become available.

By the time of the next action learning programme, the shadow set adviser is now the set adviser proper. The consultant may still be in the background, a coach and mentor, but the new set adviser is running the show. The third programme may see the consultant set adviser relegated to the role of tutor, or even to the end of a telephone line.

Organizations tend to look to training and personnel staff to provide the shadow set adviser. Certainly someone well versed in participative training and with basic facilitation skills may need less development than, say, a production engineer. For reasons discussed in Chapter 5, the latter should not be ruled out – much depends upon personal attributes.

Before we dismiss the consultant set adviser, there is one caveat, which is that there are times when the use of an external specialist is imperative – for example, when senior managers are dealing with issues which are politically sensitive, and where the involvement of an internal set adviser would be inappropriate.

In summary

We began by stating that action learning is an investment, and that there is a bottom-line return on this investment of time, energy and money. For many far-sighted companies, undertaking action learning is also an act of faith: something which is seen as the right thing to do, even though the outcome may not be quantifiable at the time the decision to go ahead is made.

After the final implementation of the recommendations of a complex action learning programme, the chief executive of a medium-sized company in a highly competitive industry commented that, looking back to where his organization was before the action learning programme began, the benefits were clearly visible. They had started by wanting to separate themselves from 'the rest of the flock'. That was what they had now done. Action learning had given them an edge that had put them far ahead of their competitors.

As we move further into the era of discontinuity, traditional approaches to dealing with issues and threats are becoming increasingly ineffective. In the situation where we cannot rely upon yesterday's experience to provide an answer to today's problems, action learning, with its ability to pose the right questions, comes into its own. The questions start with the familiar but powerful:

- What are we trying to do?
- What is stopping us?
- What can we do about it?

Action learning develops people: not just those who take part as set members, but also those who come into contact with it as tutors, clients, experts who are consulted, and all those whose views and advice are sought.

Action learning develops the set members in particular. The creation of an ERSI gives each member added confidence to practise and build on his or her personal strengths, while at the same time recognizing 'weaknesses' which have to be guarded against or offset.

Set members are also developed through the tutorials. These build on the individual's P and then encourage the set member to use this augmented P as a springboard from which to launch Q. A typical action learning programme might include the following tutorial and workshop inputs:

- project management
- team effectiveness
- managing change
- creative thinking
- time management
- effective presentations.

Unlike the normal classroom situation these inputs are needed by the set for immediate application to their project work – in fact, the inputs have been demanded by the set and have been customized to meet the set's requirements. Because of the immediate use of the learning, there is a very high level of understanding and retention.

The benefit is a more robust, flexible organization with staff who are more promotable and more capable of taking on wider responsibilities. As McGill and Beaty point out,[3] 'Managers experienced in action learning who are able to embrace variety have the skills to deal with issues rather than take the first-sighted solution.'

A very significant benefit from action learning is that it really does change the way in which the organization behaves. The paradigm of the organization – the cumulative effect of myth and anecdote ('in the old days . . .', 'remember when . . .'), routines and rituals (the dress code, the annual dinner-dance), symbols (size of office, use of dining room), control systems (monthly reports, sales targets), organizational structures (who reports to whom) – is challenged. 'This is the way we do things round here' is no longer an acceptable justification for unthinking action.

Organization development can be seen at two levels. The first comes from the challenge intrinsic in action learning, such as questioning why control systems are the way they are, why routines are sacrosanct, whether the organization structures are effective, and so on. Add to this the fact that action learning approaches problems not by a process of elimination but by generating as many alternative solutions as possible.

The second level is the cumulative action of managers who have themselves been through the action learning process and for whom the Q philosophy has become a way of life.

References

1 Peters, T. (1988), *Thriving on Chaos*, 3rd edn, London: Macmillan.
2 Morgan, G. and Ramirez, R. (1984), 'Action Learning – a holographic metaphor for guiding social change', *Human Relations* 37, pp. 1–28.
3 McGill, I. and Beaty, L. (1992), *Action Learning: a Practitioner's Guide*, London: Kogan Page.

3 Implications for the organization

So far we have discussed the nature of action learning, showing how it is project based and learner driven, produces bottom-line results by confronting significant problems and issues, and at the same time develops both individual managers and the organization itself.

In all this there are implications for the organization and aspects which, if ignored or badly handled, could damage rather than benefit the organization.

Commitment to action learning

The success of action learning depends upon the full commitment of everyone involved, whether the involvement is as a senior manager sponsoring action learning, as a set member, as a set adviser or as a client. Without this commitment the outcome will be counterproductive. Apart from a commitment to finding and implementing solutions, the set member must also be committed to his or her own personal development – and this means admitting that one is less than perfect. This may pose a stumbling-block to those who dread the prospect of having their fallibility exposed and therefore decline any invitation to join the set.

That person could be the very one who would benefit most from the action learning experience. Any undue pressure to persuade him or her to become a set member, however, could result in a disruptive set member and an ineffective set. As McGill and Beaty[1] rightly point out

Action learning is a voluntary endeavour. Being a member of a set cannot be compulsory. Membership cannot be imposed . . . we take as given that to be effective for individuals and organizations action learning needs to be based on the fundamental value that joining in, starting, being in and if necessary leaving a set is a decision for the person who wishes to be a set member. Similarly, a person who takes on the role of set adviser cannot be required or obliged to take on the role.

Although McGill and Beaty are referring to open action learning programmes where each set member is working on his or her own individual project, and where the set may be drawn from various organizations (see Chapter 9), the principle applies equally to our in-company single project action learning set.

A vulnerability of the in-company action learning programme is that employees can feel coerced to become set members. I can recall one programme which suffered badly at the outset because several set members had what they claimed to be 'grave reservations about the validity of the process'. In fact they already had very busy social lives, one working with a charity organization, another with a youth movement and a third finishing an Open University course. These activities took up much of their leisure time, and now the company in all innocence was making inroads into the little personal time they had left.

Although there was no coercion from the company, all three felt that refusing to join the action learning programme would adversely affect their career prospects.

The company's viewpoint was that those who participated in

the action learning programme became more promotable than they were before. The promotability of those who did not take part was neither enhanced nor diminished.

As it happened, one withdrew in the very early stages before the programme got under way. The other two reluctant set members initially showed a degree of passive resistance which evaporated once the set began to deal with real issues that affected them all. 'After all,' they said, 'we couldn't let the others down.'

Going back to the employee who sees the action learning programme as a threat to his or her credibility, one approach might be to unashamedly persuade him or her to join the set so that the set may benefit from his or her skills and knowledge, with the proviso that the employee can always leave if the process is found to be unbearable. Once inside the set it is highly unlikely that the employee will leave it, thanks to the bonding process that takes place there.

An alternative is to accept gracefully the many reasons why a manager cannot join the set: pressures of work, other projects, and so forth. Having accepted these reasons, the next step is to make a plea that he or she stay close, so that the set can benefit from advice and direction. Inevitably the manager discovers a compelling interest in the activities of the set. Fearful of being left out, he or she approaches the set adviser saying, in effect, 'I feel that the set really needs me, so I've rearranged my workload in order to join them.'

Supporting and caring for each other is a feature of action learning sets. The comrades in adversity quickly develop a sense of duty towards each other. During my work with MBA sets, I have known set members give up weekend after weekend (to the dismay of their families) to travel to distant meeting-places in order to help each other. This in addition to the formal scheduled set meetings.

Commitment, then, grows as the set matures, and this applies to commitment to a successful outcome as well as commitment to the set itself. An implication for the organization is that an internal network is being developed: a network of people who have been through a common experience, shared a common adversity and formed a rapport which transcends formal hierarchical relationships. The result is freer communication and greater flexibility across the organization.

Top management's commitment is a *sine qua non* for successful action learning. It is usually a senior manager who initiates action learning, having gained the support of his or her own manager. However, the demands which action learning makes upon scarce resources are often not recognized until the action learning programme is well under way.

Where successful action learning brings a whole range of benefits, unsuccessful action learning can be damagingly counterproductive. Failure usually means that the set is disbanded, individuals are demoralized, the action learning process given a bad name and any future programmes put in jeopardy. And because action learning has such high visibility, failure does not pass unnoticed.

Time

Time is a resource that comes under immediate pressure. Even in those programmes where set meetings are held half in company time and half in the set members' own time, the time pressures mount up quickly, particularly as each set member is doing his or her normal job on a day-to-day basis while working on the action learning programme. To a lesser extent this also holds true for the client.

In addition to this the set, in its quest for data, will be crossing boundaries, going into various departments to ask questions and, frequently, to observe. This again takes time, here the time (and goodwill) of those who have to answer questions and give explanations.

Returning to the commitment of top management, it is salutary to remember that if the set is going to succeed in its task it will have to be politically aware. We can reasonably expect people in the highest positions in the organization to have the most clout – the most power and influence. This clout can work for the set or against it. The secret is to make sure that the power-holders are on your side, and here the client has a key role to perform in promoting the interests of the set.

If action learning is likely to face too much opposition, if there are powerful people with vested interests in going their own way regardless, then it would be better not to launch into an action learning programme.

Communication

Communication goes hand in hand with commitment. Writing on action research (see Chapter 6), Bennett and Oliver[2] comment:

Remember, if you want people to be involved, participative, enthusiastic and committed, they need to be kept informed at a level that will allow them to be all those things. They especially need to know why the project exists, what its objectives are, and they need regular progress reports.

Communicating to the external world is a task which all action learning sets have to undertake. Set meetings will not go unnoticed: a set of six may mean six separate departments all having their work patterns disrupted regularly as a set member takes himself or herself off to a set meeting, leaving colleagues to provide the necessary cover. These colleagues at least will want to know what is going on and why.

There is a need for a continuous flow of reliable information, for progress reports at regular intervals, so that the grapevine rumours are pre-empted.

Some of the action learning sets I have worked with have issued regular newsletters. Others have made full use of in-company journals, and one went to the length of holding and videoing debriefing meetings of the 'news conference' type, with the video then being played at lunch time in a corner of the canteen. An unexpected benefit was that the debriefing sessions soon became two-way events, with the set receiving feedback from the attendees.

Having encouraged the setting up of a system for telling the organization about the purpose and progress of the action learning programme, the organization itself may be put under pressure to provide similar communication systems whenever large projects or other interventions are about to take off.

This is organizational development at work.

Openness, trust and changing relationships

The issues of commitment and communication are allied to those of trust and openness. There are two aspects: the openness and trust shown by the organization towards the set, and the extent to which the same openness and trust is seen inside the set.

One of the prerequisites of action learning is that the set members should feel relaxed and comfortable in confronting internal issues, critically discussing each others' ideas and proposals and in sharing confidential information; this is one reason why no one should be coerced into joining an action learning programme or into remaining in it against his or her will. Here the implication for the organization is that it will have to respond openly and in good faith to the comment and criticism which it in turn receives from the set.

The need for organizations to be able to respond and adapt quickly to new sets of conditions is leading to a narrowing of the gap between what used to be regarded as strategic issues and what was seen as merely operational. Despite management pundits having preached for many years that decisions should be taken at the lowest management level where all the relevant facts were available, this rarely happened. Now we are beginning to see a change. As a result of devolution and 'downsizing', information has had to be made more accessible. For the same reasons, many senior managers are having to become more and more involved in day-to-day operational matters.

In their forward-looking document *A Perspective on Personnel*,[3] the Personnel Standards Lead Body says:

Emphasis on hierarchical relationships is diminishing. They are being replaced by more informal relationships which go across internal organisational boundaries . . . .

Senior managers are looking for processes which bind the organisation together. These processes become increasingly important where organisations are devolving: adverse consequences of decentralisation must be countered with a renewed emphasis on integration, so that the different parts of the enterprise pull together to meet customer needs and to share scarce or expensive resources. These processes must encourage and align the success of the individual, the success of the team and the success of the enterprise.

The report goes on to list some of the mechanisms for achieving this integration as:

- emphasis on common culture, concepts, values, standards of behaviour and vocabulary;
- widespread and common understanding of business vision, mission, direction and strategy;
- encouragement of teamwork within the organisation, and with others from outside, such as customers, suppliers, joint-venture partners;
- open communications channels achieved through effective communications that operate both upwards and downwards as well as horizontally across organisational boundaries.

The concept that change is constant, that what worked yesterday will be of little relevance tomorrow, is at the very core of action learning. The quotations from *A Perspective on Personnel* reiterate the action learning theme: only when people within the organization have a common understanding of what the business is all about and where it is going, only when teamwork is fostered and only when the system for passing information around the organization is open and responsive can the organization itself be truly competitive in the long term.

Today's senior executives live in a world of contradictions. Devolution, for example, is leading to the setting up of more and smaller business units, but growth is still a priority for the organization. Competitive edge must be maintained by innovation, yet standardization and efficiency remain key themes.

The ability to adapt quickly to a changing environment must live side by side with demands for stability and predictability.

Action learning is able to supply a large part of the answer to the difficulties created by this dichotomous situation, P (programmed knowledge) providing the ability to exploit standardization, stability and efficiency, and Q (the questioning facility) giving the ability to respond with alacrity to changing conditions.

Action learning and the chief executive

Chief executives, particularly those who run smaller organizations, often face a dilemma. They find themselves in the situation where they want to become involved in action learning within their own organization but, for several reasons, feel themselves prevented from doing so.

The most common reason is privilege – action learning depends upon the freedom of the set members to discuss contentious and often confidential issues freely. With access to privileged information the chief executive may feel inhibited and unable to enter into too free a debate. His reservations spring from genuine and acceptable reasons – part of the 'loneliness of command'. By definition, chief executives have no peers within their own organizations. So who does the chief executive confide in when it comes to talking through the issues which confront the future of the organization?

Action learning offers an answer in the form of the open action learning set. The mechanics of an open action learning programme are described in detail in Chapter 9. In essence, the set members come from different organizations, or perhaps from different divisions of a large organization, each bringing his or her own project to be worked on. Each set member becomes a consultant, adviser and devil's advocate to every other set member. In a set of six, therefore, each set member will have five comrades in adversity, all providing support and advice throughout the programme.

The action learning principles remain the same: the quest for relevant P, the development of apposite Q, the support for each other as a learning group coping with the problem of what to do next when no one knows the way out of a complex problem.

Chief executives can flourish within this environment. I have known chief executives who have been at the same time members of an open action learning set and clients for action learning programmes within their own organizations. In one case the two projects were linked so that, while the chief executive was examining the wider, long-term implications and ramifications of a course of action, the in-company set were looking in closer detail at the short- and medium-term issues.

Senior managers, directors and chief executives, in particular, are not well catered for in terms of formal developmental opportunities. Cynics may quote the Peter Principle,[4] arguing cause and effect. The truth is simpler. For one thing, there are fewer people at the top than there are further down the managerial ladder, and less research has been carried out. In-house management trainers and educators have tended to sit beside the chief executive and look downwards, defining the needs of those below director level. Mumford, Robinson and Stradling[5] comment that: 'At the top level the thing which main board directors have to do well may have changed very substantially either by the time a manager reaches the top, or indeed after it.'

Why invest precious time and effort in learning which may prove to be irrelevant in the long term? In their recommendations on the development of directors they state that: 'The normal managerial activities of problem-solving, of working in task groups and on projects are badly under-utilised . . . . Areas such as these have a major potential for producing development without substantial extra cost.'

Bob Garratt[6] refers to four elements which, he suggests, should appear in every director's self-development plan: a personal development agenda, a director development agenda, a team development agenda and a business development agenda.

The personal agenda is concerned with behavioural aspects

of the director's performance and may include such things as hospitality skills or the ability to converse in a foreign language. The director agenda deals with becoming a general, as opposed to a specialist, manager. The team development agenda is there to help the new director become an effective member of the top decision-making, performance-monitoring team. The business development agenda, says Bob Garratt,

is the final process of integrating the previous three agendas into the objectives of the business. As such it can be highly advantageous to use an Action Learning process to achieve the necessary simultaneous developmental processes because it allows the specific issues facing a business at any one time to be addressed in a rigorous manner by the very people who will have to solve them anyway. It is a cost-effective form of development.

Costs – a perspective

It is not possible to assess accurately the costs involved in setting up and running an action learning programme – there are too many variables, and in the final analysis a successful action learning programme saves money far beyond the cost of the programme. However, it is possible to identify the main costs that an organization is likely to incur when bringing in action learning for the first time, namely:

- the cost of bringing in a consultant as set adviser,*
- costs associated with external tutors,

and to comment upon the other two main areas where expense occurs:

- the cost associated with the time employees spend on action learning,
- administrative, accommodation and other costs.

---

* See also Chapter 11, 'Set advisers' fees – a footnote'. This looks at the specific aspects of introducing action learning into small organizations.

We may start by assuming that an organization embarking on its first action learning programme will want to use an experienced consultant to be set adviser, to generally supervise the programme and be the link between the sponsor, the client and the set. In many cases the organization will also want the set adviser to train a member of its own staff to share in and eventually manage the implementation of future action learning programmes – the shadow set adviser referred to in Chapter 2 under 'Self-reliance'.

In appointing an external consultant the choice lies somewhere between individual training and development specialists operating on their own account and, at the other end of the scale, large generalist management consultancies who happen to have action learning expertise. There are also business school and university departments offering their own approaches to action learning. The practical advantages and disadvantages of each type of consultancy is discussed in detail in Chapter 9.

The result of this diversity is mirrored in the widely differing fees charged by suppliers. It is worth remembering that the fee levels do not necessarily reflect the consultants' ability to introduce and run action learning successfully, but rather the overhead and other financial commitments of the consultancy, as well as the reputation it enjoys.

At the lower end of the fee range an independent freelance training and development specialist working from a home-based office and with minimal overheads may base his charges somewhere within the range of £400 to £750 per day (1994 levels). He or she would look to the client to meet the cost of any extras, such as those associated with the cost of any external venues.

Setting a fee for an action learning programme is always difficult for the consultant until he or she has developed a feel for what is involved in a particular programme and done some initial calculations. The problem with client organizations is that they need to know the potential cost at an early stage for budgetary reasons. Feeling under pressure to give some indication to the client, a consultant may explain that his or her fees are based on so much per day – say, for example, £600. This implies that for specific short-term assignments (for example, running a three-day training event) he or she would invoice the organization for £1800, including all research and development.

Action learning rarely works this way. The £600 is merely a starting-point in the calculation. An action learning programme can be spread over six or seven months or even more, and can be full of surprises. After the decision to go ahead has been made the consultant will be involved from the very beginning in a series of short one- or two-hour meetings with managers, potential clients, set members and others. He or she will be involved for several complete days (and often nights) during the start-up of the programme and for many half days during the life of the programme.

Furthermore, there will be other whole days taken up by workshops later in the programme, as well as countless short visits to talk with people (not necessarily set members or clients). Add to this a welter of meetings with potential tutors, all of whom will have to be briefed in detail as to what exactly the set needs.

Action learning, as we have said, is learner driven, so the consultant must be prepared to devote time to meeting (usually at very short notice) the set's innumerable requests for tutors, contacts and sources of information.

All this takes time, and time is the only commodity a consultant has to sell. If a consultant is let down by a client at short notice he cannot put Tuesday the 14th back into stock and sell it again the following week. So he must calculate carefully, trying to foresee all eventualities in an unpredictable situation, while at the same time giving the client as accurate a picture as possible of the costs involved.

Coming back to our freelance training and development consultant, let us assume that he or she takes £600 per day as a basis for calculating fees. From experience the consultant may predict being involved in the action learning programme outlined in Figure 6.1 (p. 101) for the following number of days:

meetings prior to start-up	3 days
start-up workshop	3 days
set meetings (say 16 × ½ days)	8 days
2 workshops	4 days
Subtotal	18 days

In addition there are days spent off site working on the client's behalf:

Selecting and briefing tutors	4 days
Developing inputs, administration, etc.	2 days
Total	24 days

The resultant figure of £14,400 will in all probability be discounted by the independent consultant. Because marketing costs are so disproportionately high for the small consultancy, independent consultants are normally interested in developing long-term relationships and in getting business through referrals.

Where the fees of freelance independent consultants may range from below £400 to above £1000 per day, the large management consultancy groups tend to start around the £1250 per day figure. The fee structure of business school and university-based consultants is generally in line with that of independent consultants. But there are exceptions, particularly when it is the business school itself, rather than an independent group of individuals within it, which is going to run the programme. Business schools, and consultants based within them, may have a different motivation from other types of consultancies, and their priorities should be taken into consideration.

The other fees which have to be paid by the client organization are for tutorials given by external tutors. It is normal for the set adviser to select the external tutor and brief him or her. The fee is usually the same as, or less than, the set adviser's daily rate. A tutorial will usually last for up to two hours, with the tutor spending the next two hours or more working with the set. The invoice will therefore be for a half-day's fee, unless teaching in a workshop has been involved.

Returning to our calculation based on Figure 6.1, this now looks like:

fees for set adviser	£10,800
start-up workshop (1½ days)	900*
Twelve tutorials (12 × ½ day)	3,600
two skills workshops (2 × 2 days)	2,400†
Total	£17,700

The other cost which is often quoted is the imponderable one: the cost to the organization of the man-hours spent by employees on the action learning programme. There is an erroneous assumption that all employees are intensely occupied furthering their employer's business 100 per cent of the time they are at work. To reduce this to 50 per cent would still be to err generously. In fact, in most action learning programmes the set members donate large amounts of their personal time to both formal and informal meetings. It would therefore seem unrealistic to include a figure for 'lost time' when calculating the costs of an action learning programme.

Because action learning takes place as far as possible on site there are few hotel or conference centre costs. The exception is the start-up workshop where there are distinct advantages in going off site.

In Chapter 1 we saw how large sets could be formed into smaller sub-sets to achieve working groups of between four and eight members. An experienced set adviser can work with two or even three sets at the same time. In terms of the action learning model we are discussing – an in-company programme with each set or sub-set tackling one issue – under the right conditions one set adviser working with up to 24 set members is just feasible, although very hard work for the set adviser. If we also assume that there is sufficient affinity between the issues being addressed to allow all the sets to share tutorials, we can take our calculated cost of £17,700 to represent a cost of

---

* Fees for tutor working with set adviser.
† Assumes workshops tutored by set adviser.

less than £750 per set member. This for a substantial developmental programme spread over seven months. In 1994 £750 would just about buy one place on a three-day, non-residential, run-of-the-mill public training course.

The second time the organization runs an action learning programme the cost will be considerably less due to the in-house experience and expertise built up during the first programme, and the reduced need to buy in external expertise.

Action learning is flexible. We have concentrated on an in-house, one-problem-per-set approach. However, Chapter 9, in dealing with alternative action learning models, shows how organizations can group together to share costs.

The implication for any organization is that in action learning there is a means for developing people at all levels from shop-floor to boardroom. There are, of course, many things which action learning cannot provide, and there are many instances in which action learning would be inappropriate, but where action learning is appropriate it can revolutionize the way in which an enterprise goes about its business.

In the 1960s, the expression 'management by objectives' (MBO) was in vogue. Its concepts of agreeing objectives and targets, and of quantifying and qualifying, were a revelation to many organizations, which set about applying them with gusto. Today we seldom hear anyone talk about management by objectives. We do not need to. MBO has become so deeply enmeshed in our everyday management practices that it is simply the way companies run their businesses.

Similarly, techniques such as value engineering, all the rage in the 1970s, are today part of accepted wisdom and therefore anonymous.

Could it be that action learning will one day attain similar anonymity, absorbed into the sinews of corporate life?

References

1   McGill, I. and Beaty, L. (1992), *Action Learning: a Practitioner's Guide*, London: Kogan Page.

2   Bennett, R. and Oliver, J. (1988), *How to Get the Best from Action Research – a Guidebook*, Bradford: MCB University Press.
3   Personnel Standards Lead Body (1993), *A Perspective on Personnel*, London: Employment Department. This material is Crown Copyright and is reproduced here by permission of the Employment Department.
4   Peter, L. J. and Hull, R. (1969), *The Peter Principle*, London: Souvenir.
5   Mumford, A., Robinson G. and Stradling, D. (1987), *Developing Directors – The Learning Process*, Sheffield: MSC. Crown copyright. Reproduced with permission of the Controller of Her Majesty's Stationery Office.
6   Garratt, R. (1987), *The Learning Organisation*, Aldershot: Gower.

Part 2
Making Action Learning Work

4 Preparing for action learning

Action learning brings people together to undertake projects. The purpose is twofold: the development of the people (and thereby the organization) on the one hand, and on the other the solving of problems and issues of import to the organization.

In most cases the employees who form the set are unlikely to have worked in an action learning programme before. They will therefore need help and guidance from an 'expert' who knows all about the action learning process and whose job it is to guide them through to a successful conclusion. This expert, the set adviser, may have no knowledge of the organization, the industry it is in or the customers it serves, but what the set adviser does bring is the ability to help the group achieve its purposes.

The problem which the set confronts does not exist in isolation. Some manager within the organization owns it, and others are affected by it.

In three short paragraphs we have brought together four of the constituents of most action learning programmes:

- the problem (which is to be restated as a project);

55

- the client (the person who owns the problem);
- the set members (the people on the project team);
- the set adviser (the action learning expert).

To this list we can add the tutors (subject-matter specialists, both internal and external) to complete the list of essential elements. Each of these needs to be examined carefully before we go ahead with an action learning programme.

Selecting the project

There is a great deal of overlap between the terms 'problem', 'issue' and 'project'. A project cannot exist unless there is a problem to be solved, and problems themselves are the result of unresolved issues. For the sake of readability, the three terms are frequently interchangeable.

It is often the urgency of having to do something about a pressing problem that triggers the introduction of action learning. In our refinery example (see Chapter 1) it was the difficulties that the maintenance department were having, and the consequent effect upon production, that led to an action learning programme.

In the case of a small graphic design company it was the threat of imminent closure that made the owners look to action learning for a way to solve their immediate problems and at the same time prepare them for what lay beyond. Similarly it was the need to adapt that led a large London borough council to use action learning to design and implement far-reaching changes in the way it related to the community it served.

Projects do not, however, always select themselves. Quite often it is the symptoms of a problem which are identified long before the problem itself is recognized. Action learning is concerned with tackling the problem and the underlying issues, not with papering over the cracks. Thus the nature of the problem has to be taken into account in order to determine whether or not it provides a suitable vehicle for action learning. A further criterion is that the scale of the problem to be confronted must be matched to the abilities of the set. The process of collecting and analysing information, generating and evaluating possible solutions, should stretch each set member intellectually without threatening him or her with the prospect of failure. Success is the greatest motivator we know. As managers and educators we should be engineering meaningful success for those under our tutelage.

Action learning projects can range from the operational to the strategic – a glance at those listed in Appendix 2 will show just how wide the range is. Ambiguity, however, is of the essence. Ambiguity in this context means that the project is capable of having many solutions. Where this ambiguity exists the set is forced to debate and defend several competing courses of action until critical evaluation leads them to agree on one solution. This is more than a safeguard for the quality of the decision: it is fundamental to the learning process.

Action learning projects can also be considered in terms of the setting and of the task itself, using the concept of 'familiar' as opposed to 'unfamiliar'. The refinery example was one of foremen working on familiar problems within a familiar environment. In the case of the small graphic design company the environment was familiar, but to both sets the task was unfamiliar: the set composed of sales and support staff looked at design issues, while the set of designers probed into marketing and administrative issues.

David Boddy[1] states that:

The project is a central and distinctive element in action learning. Its use reflects a basic theoretical assumption that the experienced manager will learn best when he is testing his existing ideas against a real managerial situation, and reorganizing his ideas in the light of this experience. How much a participant learns from an action learning programme is therefore assumed to depend heavily (though not solely) on the opportunities for learning which can be generated by the project.

The level of challenge presented by the action learning project must be carefully gauged. Above all, the project must be capable of having a successful outcome, and the set must be capable of achieving it. Every set member should be capable of making a significant contribution (though not necessarily to the technical aspects of the project). Stretching the individual intellectually is part of the personal development process. Demoralizing a set member by allowing him or her to be put in an intolerable position where he or she cannot make a positive contribution will damage the set, perhaps terminally.

In considering whether a project is suitable for action learning we should check whether it is feasible in the light of the skills and abilities of the set, whether its successful conclusion will bring about substantial change, and whether it offers sufficient challenge without being threatening. Other main considerations will be the extent to which the project lends itself to new ideas being generated and evaluated, as well as the extent to which set members will be exposed to new ways of thinking through set work, tutorials, action research and the crossing of functional and other boundaries.

Action learning projects must be for real. Action learning is concerned with real people working in real time on real problems. Projects which are invented for the occasion, or which have already been solved and are therefore no more than case studies, will not serve for action learning, if only because in action learning there is an explicit contract between the set and the organization that the final recommendations will be implemented.

There are two roads into action learning: the first is where the organization is faced with a problem and, having looked at the various ways in which to answer the problem, has decided that the action learning route is the most productive one to follow. Apart from arriving at a solution to the problem, staff will be developed and consultancy fees kept to a minimum.

Other organizations start from the realization that it is an effective way of making the organization more responsive to change, and thus more competitive. The difficulty that these organizations meet is deciding upon a problem which will make a suitable platform for action learning, one which will meet all the project selection criteria.

Problems can be classified as 'operational' or as 'strategic'.

Operational problems tend to be self-evident: the symptoms can be clearly seen, causing a variety of knock-on problems elsewhere. Strategic problems often go unnoticed, conspicuous by their absence – until the crunch comes.

'We do not know whether we should set up a European organization' typifies a strategic issue, as does 'We have no idea what our product range should look like three years from now'. Action learning lends itself well to these strategic problems. Action learning is concerned with opening up debate, with extending horizons by generating a diversity of ideas. Only at a later stage does it move into the detailed evaluation which so often kills off new ideas before they can be explored and their potential tapped.

Appendix 2 lists some typical action learning projects, dealing with strategic issues – for example, those concerned with:

- Corporate venturing strategies within a chemical company;
- Strategies for growth within a small development company;
- Manufacturing strategies from 1992 onwards;
- Competitive business strategies after deregulation;
- Business strategy in relation to a major account.

One difficulty with strategy-based projects is the time factor. Implementation may take place long after the action learning set has submitted its recommendations and has been disbanded. Another is that set members may too easily be seduced by philosophical argument and intellectual debate. It would follow that those who are to be set members for a project of this nature should be drawn from senior management and those who will benefit from exposure to this level of thinking.

'We do not how to set up a European organization' is, of course, an operational issue. Projects centred on operational issues have the advantages of tangibility. Philosophical debate is still encouraged, but at the end of the allocated time span recommendations have to be submitted and implementation has to start.

The chief executive, or the training and development

manager, who has decided that action learning is the way forward for his or her organization may not be able to identify personally a significant problem to translate into an action learning project. The approach here is to look at the breadth of action learning. Problems exist across all the functions in the organization, and listening to departmental managers and internal specialists can give insights into a whole range of issues.

Bear in mind, too, that because action learning projects are real they are also dynamic. As information comes to light during the course of data collection and action research, so the objectives of the project may change. In many cases it is the external environment that changes during the life of the project. In other cases it may be the realization that what were held as realistic organizational objectives at the beginning of the programme are later recognized as untenable.

Selecting the set

The type of action learning programme we are concentrating our attention on (each set or sub-set addressing a single problem) suggests that there are certain criteria to be met in putting together a set which will be successful both as a learning community and as a problem-solving team. We should, for example, include:

- those with some directly relevant technical knowledge;
- those with 'associated' technical knowledge;
- those who are there for their own general development;
- those who are in the set for specific development.

These are the more obvious selection criteria: we want to use action learning to solve our problems and at the same time provide a developmental opportunity for our people. Hence there is a balance between those who are going to make immediate technical contributions and those who, unencumbered by a technical background, will later move the project forward by using Q.

Action learning sets have been known to run successfully without a strong technical presence – technical expertise abounds in most organizations, it is simply a matter of tapping into it. It is not lack of technical know-how that forces companies out of business, but usually the lack of managerial prowess. Having a technical expert within the set may save time initially, but does not necessarily add to the quality of the result.

Those with associated technical knowledge will probably come from departments or disciplines which will be directly affected by the outcome of the project. In a project relating to sales, for example, departments such as marketing, distribution, production and research may be represented in the set. In one dealing with finance the range might be all-embracing.

The third group, those who are invited to join the set as part of their personal development, usually have a comparatively smaller contribution to make during the first few weeks of the action learning programme (unless they happen to have first-hand knowledge of the subject of the project). They are likely to spend the first few meetings learning from their fellow set members about the nature of the problem within the wider context of the whole organization and the industry in general. Once they have acclimatized themselves to the set and to the project they will make their contributions by skilful use of Q: intelligent people asking ingenuous questions, searchingly.

There may be fewer people in the fourth group. This is where an employee is destined to take over a new, usually higher-level, job at unexpectedly short notice. The new job may demand a wider understanding of both the company and the industry, coupled with a more considered approach to organizational problems. For example, the organization may want to move a specialist into a managerial role or promote a manager from departmental to general management responsibilities. Several people may be involved in the chain of moves that dominoes through the organization. Action learning can provide the accelerated personal development that each of them needs.

So far we have discussed what set members may offer in the

way of knowledge and expertise. There are, however, other considerations: the intrinsic qualities which each person brings into the team situation. In Chapter 5 we shall see how Belbin's Self-Perception Inventory[2] is used during the start-up work-shop to give the set members an insight into what makes some teams successful while others fail.

What Belbin has to tell us is that we each bring a differing set of personal attributes into the team. For a team to be successful these attributes, or work preferences, must be in balance. If they are not in balance naturally, the team must work harder to ensure that deficiencies are offset and that a surfeit of strengths in any one area is not allowed to become counterproductive. What football team would field eleven defenders, or eleven attackers?

Belbin has identified nine team roles:

The plant is an ideas person and is the team's source of original ideas and suggestions. The plant has no monopoly of creative ideas, but what does distinguish him or her is the radical nature and originality of ideas which he or she puts forward. The plant is concerned with fundamentals and significant issues, not with mundane practicalities. Plants are unconventional, dislike rules and regulations, are careless with detail work, and consequentially are often undervalued.

The resource investigator is the contacts person for the set. He or she goes outside the set to bring back information, ideas and developments. Salespeople, diplomats, liaison officers fall into this role type. Again an ideas person, but without the radical originality of the plant.

The co-ordinator is the group leader by consent. Relaxed and unassertive, he or she is concerned with leading the set in such a way that harmony and co-operation prevail. With excellent communication skills, the co-ordinator is a very good listener.

The shaper shapes the behaviour of others in order to get the task done and deadlines met. He or she unites the ideas and objectives of the team, turning them into action. Where the co-ordinator leads the group by a process of social co-ordination, the shaper has an overwhelming compulsion to achieve targets even if this means upsetting people.

The monitor–evaluator is the critic within the set, drawing attention to flaws and potential difficulties, and preventing the plant from following too many flights of fancy. The monitor–evaluator has good analytical skills.

The completer–finisher is concerned with fine detail and the tying up of loose ends. He or she dislikes disorder, preferring to see one task completed before the next is embarked upon. There is nothing easygoing about the completer–finisher when it comes to finishing the task.

The implementer is the one who gets things done, translating the set's strategies into a feasible schedules. They are seen as sincere and trustworthy, and their many personal contacts across the organization means that they know what goes on and where.

The team worker is the person who binds the team together. Likeable and unassertive, he or she is the most active communicator within the set. Importantly, team workers use their skills to maintain harmony within the set when this is threatened.

The specialist is a role which Belbin included only after he recognized that there was one type of person who did not fall convincingly into the original eight roles. This person tends to be wrapped up in a task, trade or profession, and makes very little contribution to teamwork outside his or her technical expertise. The role is only marginally pertinent to action learning.

The above short descriptions are only glimpses at the team roles. One important point is that people may be effective or non-effective in these roles, with totally different results. A shaper who is effective is essential to any team, driving forward and keeping the team's attention focused on the goal. A non-effective shaper can be a disaster, and will be seen as a tyrant or petty dictator. An effective completer–finisher is a godsend to the set. An ineffective one will bog the set down in small detail, depressing others and clouding the objectives.

Having a well-balanced team is important. Imagine what might happen in a set dominated by a surplus of shapers, each pushing to have his or her opinions accepted. Or picture a preponderance of plants, with fresh and radical ideas spinning off in all directions to the consternation of those who merely want progress and results.

Self-awareness is half the battle. When a set realizes where its weaknesses lie, be they weaknesses of scarcity or of overabundance, it can take positive steps to safeguard against any potential risks. Knowing that there is a lack of completer–finisher attributes, the set may choose to assign certain members to look after these aspects, consciously disciplining themselves to make sure that progress is on schedule and all the loose ends tidied up.

The results of the self-perception inventory show that most people score highly on three roles, and have minimal scores on one or two. Thus even in an action learning set of five people it is quite likely that all eight team roles (we exclude the specialist) will be present.

Hierarchical structure frequently comes into consideration when an in-company action learning set is being formed. Is there a risk of 'junior' staff deferring to more senior managers? Will the more junior feel inhibited in the presence of their seniors? What about issues of confidentiality? My own experience is that these are imagined rather than real problems. One governing factor is the culture of the organization. We have already seen that the trend is for hierarchical structure to collapse as working units become smaller, communication more flexible and information more freely available.

The first time the set meet in a working situation is at the start-up workshop (see Chapter 5). Here the experience of working together in areas where no one person has hierarchical authority breaks down existing perceived barriers and binds the set together.

Selecting the set adviser

The set adviser may come from within the organization or may be an external specialist (a consultant) who has built up an expertise in running action learning programmes.

There are two situations in particular which call for the services of an experienced external consultant. The first is when the organization is embarking upon action learning for the first time. The second is when there are issues of confidentiality, with perhaps the chief executive and other senior managers making up the set.

We saw earlier that set advisers fall into three main groupings: small (often one person) consultancies, large management consultancies and university or business schools. Each type of consultancy has its own peculiar advantages and disadvantages. With the small consultancy what you see is what you get. With a large management consultancy you may see and be impressed by the consultant who sells the programme, but what you get as set adviser may be a much more junior person.

The gap in resources between a large consultancy and, say, a consultant working by himself or herself is not as wide as you may imagine. A large consultancy will have consultants on the payroll and they will understandably want to use these consultants as tutors whenever possible. The lone consultant will have an extensive network of self-employed associates specializing in their own subjects and each one anxious to perform well regardless of the time spent in research and preparation – after all, most of their business comes from referrals.

Universities and business schools provide a different dimension. The faculty members who will be involved in the action learning programme may well be looking to the organization to provide a fecund field for paid research, while the institution itself may be trying to establish or extend its credibility in the business community. Although training and management consultants may frequently intellectualize, they are seldom academic in their approach. College-based consultants are often academic and are usually more at home in the 'open' set situation than in the cut and thrust of the more pragmatic in-company, one-project-per-set environment.

So in choosing a set adviser it is worth examining both the resources the consultant can muster and the type of action learning experience he or she has had.

What, then, are the qualities and attributes of the ideal set adviser for our in-company programme? Perhaps an understanding of business in general heads the list, together with the ability to see the overall picture. This requirement would rule out those with too narrow an upbringing, and suggests that maturity in organizational affairs and experience in a range of disciplines at policy-making level is needed.

Being well connected is another necessity – in effect, having the wide network of associates referred to earlier who between them can deliver all but the most unusual tutorial inputs. Being well connected also means having an entrée into other organizations from which tutors may be plucked or to which set members can be sent to carry out action research (see Chapter 6). The third aspect of being well connected is that of knowing how to access data.

Good interpersonal skills are indispensable. The set adviser is going to spend a considerable amount of time influencing people within the set, within the organization and outside. One difference between being a set adviser and a facilitator is that the set adviser occasionally has to be directive (anathema to the true facilitator). The set adviser is the ultimate enforcer of the discipline of action learning and from time to time has to be firm about output, quality of work and the meeting of deadlines. The set adviser is also a counsellor, supportive and non-judgmental.

A point easy to overlook is that action learning, being learner driven, is unpredictable. The set can and does call for the unforeseen, and can rightly expect the call to be serviced with alacrity. What happens when the set adviser's diary is booked solid, with every hour of every day accounted for over the next six months? And what about the urgent but unscheduled cries for help from the set and from the client?

Above all, the set adviser must be responsive to the set's needs. An effective set adviser earnestly wants people to learn. Many trainers simply want to teach. These are the ones who have great difficulty in adopting the low profile that is usually the lot of set advisers during the final stages of an action learning programme. It is particularly true of those trainers who have developed and relied upon what are known in training jargon as 'facilitating' skills.

Beware of the set adviser who is prepared to deliver all tutorials personally. Normally it is part of the set adviser's duties to tutor in his or her own field as well as to be the guru of action learning. I have, however, come across a situation where a very capable training consultant with an impressive management background in finance and in marketing, has, by dint of experience plus an MBA, undertaken competently all the tutorials demanded by his set.

My point is that in action learning a large part of the learning comes from the set's exposure to different tutors from differing backgrounds and with differing points of view. Action learning is learning from others, and the more others the better.

Once an organization has decided to invest in action learning it makes sound sense for it to appoint the set adviser as early as possible. In most instances where an external set adviser is to be used, this will be the consultant who helped the organization make the decision. A good set adviser will be able to lead the organization through the maze of issues which have to be attended to before the start-up workshop – issues such as selecting the problem, the client and the set.

Selecting the client

Normally it is the person who owns the problem, wants it solved and has instigated action that becomes the client.

Usually the client is at a higher management level than the most senior set members. In all cases, the client has a vested interest in securing a workable solution to the problem.

We have emphasized throughout that in action learning there is a contract between the set and the organization that the findings of the set will be implemented. It is up to the client to make sure that the recommendations are, in fact, feasible and workable. Using his or her broader knowledge of the problems involved and a greater sensitivity to political issues, the client prevents the set from embarking upon a course of action which he or she knows will be fruitless.

In order to promote the interests of the set the client must have credibility and be well regarded by fellow managers and decision-makers, able to persuade and influence them in the set's interests. In addition to all this the client must be enthusiastic about the potential of action learning, and have the support of his or her own manager. Being a client is not a sinecure.

Perhaps the greatest difficulty for most managers in the client role is the need to be non-directive. The client must strike a fine balance between pointing the set in the right direction and pushing them down a preordained path. Like the set adviser, the client is intimately related to the set but not part of it. Like the set adviser, the client must seek to widen the set's thinking, helping them to open up fresh options. And again like the set adviser, the client must be prepared to listen: ego trips are out.

While in most instances there is a natural choice of client (the person who owns the problem and wants it solved) there are times when we have to go further afield to find the most appropriate choice. On one occasion the chief executive of a company employing some six hundred people decided, in conjunction with his senior managers, that action learning offered an ideal way of tackling three closely related and far-reaching problems. Having decided that the action learning set should consist of four of his senior managers plus three middle managers he then found himself torn between being a set member and becoming the client (he did think about, but dismissed, the idea of being both). In the end his own manager at group director level became the client, leaving him free to become an enthusiastic set member.

In smaller organizations it is not uncommon for the client to be a set member. Although this may seem to simplify the process of implementation it does mean that the set adviser and the set itself must be on guard against any tendency to comply too readily with the client's suggestions. It puts the onus upon the client not to stifle learning opportunities by closing down options prematurely.

In selecting the client we are looking for someone who really does want a solution to the problem and who is prepared to invest time and effort in making it possible for the set to put forward feasible recommendations. Above all, we need a client who is in sympathy with the learning needs of the set members, who will not be over-prescriptive, and who, ideally, has the power to see that the set's carefully considered recommendations are implemented.

The learning log – a crucial consideration

A core factor affecting the design of an in-company action learning programme is the balance in emphasis between the people development aspect and the need to reach a solution to the problem.

Some organizations start from: 'We want to develop our managers and staff, and if we can solve some of our major problems in the process we shall be delighted.' Others say: 'We need an answer to this issue: wouldn't it be a great idea to get some of our own people to tackle it and maybe learn something in the process.'

One significant difference in these approaches is the use (or non-use) of the learning log. The learning log is discussed in greater detail in Chapter 5. Not to insist upon the use of a learning log is an easy option – after all, supervisors and managers tend to be activist and pragmatist in their learning styles, and as such will see keeping a learning log as a tedious chore with little end value. It is only the comparative few who have a well-developed reflector learning style who will immediately see the benefits of the learning log and enjoy keeping one.

Paradoxically, I have seen MBA students, all experienced managers from industry and commerce, initially revolt at the suggestion of keeping a learning log, and then, after a few months, come to regard the log as a very personal and cherished learning tool which they have carried with them back into their daily working life.

Without the learning log many learning opportunities are lost, either because the opportunity was not recognized in the first place, or reflected upon in the second.

The learning log is central to the action learning philosophy and should only be dispensed with in exceptional circumstances. The decision whether or not logbooks are to be kept is one that should be taken before the programme starts so that ample time for discussing both learning styles and learning logs can be built into the start-up workshop.

A successful way of ensuring that learning logs are kept and used is to have, at the final presentation to the client and his guests, a short résumé by each set member of the learning he or she has acquired in the course of the programme, based upon his or her learning log entries.

Proclaiming the programme

In the previous chapter we stressed how important it was that not only the existence but also the activities of the set were made known to the organization at large.

At this preparatory stage there are no activities to report, only decisions and intentions: for example, the fact that an action learning set is being put together, why, and who is in the set. This will naturally raise the question, 'What is action learning?' The reply is difficult. In a short space of time we have to give those who may very well become involved in the programme an understanding of the key features of action learning.

Many organizations have gone to considerable lengths to make sure that people were made aware of what the company was trying to achieve, and how. A practice which seems to be growing is for the organization to announce the introduction of action learning, and then give a series of presentations explaining the key concepts of action learning, with question and answer sessions at the end. Frequently the presentations, complete with question and answer sessions, are put on videotape and sent to other branches or divisions of the organization.

Certainly the presentations and the videotapes leave many questions unanswered. But they do generate an awareness that change is happening, that it is overt, and that many employees at all levels will be able to contribute.

References

1 Boddy, D. (1981), 'Putting Action Learning into Action', *Journal of European Industrial Training*, vol. 5, no. 5, Bradford: MCB–University Press.
2 Belbin, R. M. (1981), *Management Teams, Why They Succeed or Fail*, London: Heinemann.

5 The start-up workshop

At last, after weeks of planning and preparation, the big day arrives. The start-up workshop begins and the action learning programme is under way.

Despite previous meetings in small groups, this will probably be the first time the set has come together with an agenda to work through. Several of the set members may well have worked as colleagues in the past, but this time the task is new and relationships have to be established. However good pre-workshop briefings may have been they will all have been waiting for this day, not quite sure what is going to happen to them or what is going to be expected from them.

The purpose of the start-up workshop

The start-up workshop has to achieve several results in a relatively short period – usually two to three days.

Perhaps the main concern of the start-up workshop is to give participants an understanding of the principal concepts of action learning. From there the set adviser can enlarge upon

73

the implications for the set and the opportunities for personal growth and development. If we are asking our employees to go through the action learning experience, we should provide them with the opportunity to hear what the organization intends for them and with the chance to formulate and ask questions.

To help set members develop and make new and significant contributions to the work of the set we have to increase their self-awareness, giving them an understanding of their own individual strengths and (for want of a more appropriate word) weaknesses. We also want them to work cohesively and effectively as a team. The start-up workshop caters for the former by devoting time to an examination of individual learning styles (see Chapter 1), stressing the affinity between learning theory and action learning. Belbin's self-perception inventory and theory of team roles (see Chapter 4) is one model which can be used at this juncture to introduce the concept of team roles and individual work preferences.

A fundamental task for any start-up workshop is to get the set to design the project and the means of controlling its progress. However, before the set can embark upon this activity there is the crucial stage of defining *exactly* what the problem is. This leads to several discussions between the set and the client, after which all agree on a written definition of the problem. And before they can start on the project proper, the set must translate this problem definition into a written project statement – again, agreed with the client.

Once the project statement has been agreed upon the set will need to draw up a timetable to work to if they are to manage the progress of the project work. The design and management of projects is a vital part of the start-up workshop. Having been exposed to the basics of project management the set produce their first bar charts (and even critical-path networks) from which to monitor and control progress.

The start-up workshop also deals with the mundane realities of action learning: where shall the set meet, when and how often? Time is needed for these deliberations. Diaries, holidays and other commitments come into the equation.

We can use behavioural terms to summarize the purpose of the start-up workshop. At the end of the workshop, the set will have:

- gained an understanding of the basic concepts and mechanics of action learning;
- agreed with the client a definition of the problem;
- translated the problem into a project statement and agreed this statement with the client;
- produced a critical-path network or a bar chart showing proposed completion dates for critical points in the progress of the project;
- identified resources (e.g. tutorials, workshops, contacts) which will be needed;
- agreed domestic and administrative procedures – such as where, when and how often to meet;
- acquired an increased self-awareness which will enable them individually to contribute effectively to set meetings;
- gained an understanding of learning theory and learning styles which will allow it to exploit the development opportunities offered by the action learning programme.

In effect, the purpose of the start-up workshop is to prime the set so that they are able to come to grips with the project and their own development, with help from the set adviser and support from the client.

Figure 5.1 shows a typical programme for an action learning start-up workshop. The subject-matter is designed to meet the immediate needs of the set and falls into the main areas of action learning theory, learning styles and learning logs, team effectiveness, and project design and management. The set also has to reach agreement on administrative and domestic issues such as how long the project should take to complete, and where, when and how often to hold their formal set meetings. The start-up workshop is partly an information-gathering meeting and partly a decision-making one. Normally the only administrative decision made by the organization is the date and duration of the start-up workshop. During the workshop the set members take over and make their own plans.

Launching the workshop

The start-up workshop may be opened by the chief executive or, if the chief executive is otherwise involved in the programme as client or set member, by an even more senior personage. Otherwise, and frequently, it may be the set adviser aided by the client.

Beware, however, of the situation where the chief executive arrives at the last moment, talks generalities for fifteen minutes and is then whisked away in a long limousine to attend what is ostensibly an even more important function. If this happens the fault lies not in the chief executive but in the set adviser who has failed to make the chief executive understand that merely going through the motions serves only to harm the action learning programme. The client and the set adviser are left to persuade the set that the organization is fully committed to implementing the results of the programme.

When a manager of appropriately senior status attends the opening of the workshop, is seen to be briefed and supportive, and is willing to spend time with the set – not necessarily opening the proceedings – the set sense that the programme is being taken seriously. However, there is one caveat: sporadic appearances during social interludes are more welcome than one prolonged visit. Much of the work the set has to get through is of a personal nature, and the presence of influential senior people, however well intentioned, can be inhibiting.

The content of the start-up workshop

Action learning
The participants will want to know what they have let themselves in for. During the preliminary talks with individuals and small groups of potential set members the set

Time	Evening 1	Day 1	Day 2
0800 – 1230		Introduction to action learning Learning styles Learning logs	Review day 1 Problem definition Project statement
1230 – 1315		Lunch	Lunch
1315 – 1730		Team effectiveness Project design and management	Project scheduling and resource allocation Logistics and domestic issues
1800 – 2000	Welcome Introductions Background	Team exercise	

Figure 5.1 Typical two-day residential start-up workshop

adviser will have described the basic concepts. Now is the opportunity to set everything in context. Action learning must be seen as totally relevant not only to individual learning needs but also to the needs of the organization.

My own approach, aided by overhead transparencies, is to start by showing and defining action learning as $L = P + Q$. This has immediate impact. What some felt was going to be a 'soft' subject has suddenly taken on a structure, a substance. When they hear that the perpetrator of the equation is himself a physicist by training, the technically biased are duly impressed.

Elaborating on the equation takes us directly into a consideration of the nature of P and Q. Thus we are straight into the heart of action learning.

To give the set a more focused view of action learning I explain that action learning is about project teams called 'sets' which meet regularly on a formal basis to work together, and that the task of a set is to find solutions to one or more significant problems facing the organization. Equally, action learning is concerned with helping individual set members to learn and develop through a social process.

I go on to stress that they, the set, are in the driving seat. Action learning is learner driven.

Before breaking off for discussion I talk about the benefits which action learning offers individuals and organizations, summarizing these as:

- the bottom-line benefits through solutions to problems;
- more effective and promotable employees;
- the ability to respond quickly to change;
- the acquisition of a powerful problem-solving tool.

After the question and answer session we move on to put more flesh on the bare bones of action learning. I begin by looking at the distinguishing features of action learning. Sets must be composed of employees investigating real problems, in the here-and-now. Projects which are put together for training and development purposes may be fine, but they are far removed from the reality of action learning.

Action learning centres on Q. This does not mean that P is discounted. Far from it: no organization will attain the leading edge if it does not make the best use of the latest in P. In action learning we build on P, using it as a springboard from which to launch into Q.

Action learning sets must be able to call upon the assistance of internal and external tutors and specialists. Set members must be free to discuss suggestions, and support and advise each other as comrades in adversity. Action learning sets have a set adviser at their disposal to help them through the learning process and make contacts for them. They also have a client who needs them to succeed, who can oil political wheels for them and who can ensure the acceptability of their recommendations.

By now the realization has dawned that this is a well thought out process which leaves little to chance and which will stretch them intellectually.

Importantly, examples of when not to use action learning follow – for instance, when the answer exists somewhere in P, and can be unearthed by detailed analysis. Or when there is not enough openness in the organization. Or when autocratic decisions are bound to prevail, regardless.

As I am talking to members of an organization already committed to action learning these points become academic, but they do reinforce the morale of the set, even in the face of the in-house comedians.

Finally I talk the set through the stages of the action learning programme (see Chapter 6) from start-up to final presentation to the client. Although it may all sound strange and confusing at this stage, I shall be there to guide them as set adviser through the maze. The onus is upon them to make the best use of my skills and experience.

Learning styles

In Chapter 1 we discussed Kolb's learning cycle and went on to look at the development of this model in the UK by Peter

Honey and Alan Mumford. To give set members an understanding of their own individual learning styles I start by asking them to complete and score the Learning Styles Questionnaire (LSQ). They then post the results on a flipchart (I have previously obtained the set's agreement that they will share this information).

The next step is to get each set member to identify two learning experiences which were effective and enjoyable, and two which were ineffective (a waste of time) and not enjoyable. They are asked to make notes on why these experiences were good or bad.

Before discussing the results I move on to the theory of learning style, eventually returning to the LSQ scores on the flipchart and examining various implications. Then, armed with the set's recollections of effective and ineffective experiences, it is usually a simple matter to relate the theory to the realities of the past.

However, this is retrospective. My aim now is to point the set members towards the future. Knowing their preferred learning styles they should plan to learn accordingly, using their preferred styles whenever possible. They should also plan to learn from experiences that they are going to have. Learning from experience can be proactive, and much more effective than the haphazard experiential learning of the past.

This leads naturally to a discussion on the type of learning opportunities which are likely to arise in the course of the action learning programme, and eventually to the learning log (see Chapter 4).

The learning log

As we saw in the previous chapter, keeping a learning log is one way of making sure that each significant experience is recorded and reflected upon. It may be days or weeks after the event before we are able to fit what we have learnt into our overall philosophy, and even longer before we have an opportunity to put the outcome to the test. Unless we keep a log, however, it is unlikely that we shall consciously move from the hands-on experience (activist) to reflect upon it (reflector) and then conceptualize (theorist) before finally trying out our new response to similar events (pragmatist).

The learning log is an integral component of action learning. Organizations which run action learning programmes where there is no necessity for the set members to keep learning logs lose one of the most powerful long-term benefits of action learning, to the detriment of both the business and the individual set member.

There is a tendency for some organizations to introduce action learning on the cheap. 'Action learning is being misused by employers as cheap training option' was a caption in the May 1993 issue of *Personnel Management*. The report went on to say that some organizations saw action learning, with its problem-solving, project-based approach, as a way of saving time and money. They did not understand the demands of action learning. A survey carried out in Australia showed that the main cause of failure among action learning programmes was that organizations did not appreciate that learning takes time.

One way of cutting back on cost may appear to be to concentrate on the project task at the expense of the learning element – but the eventual price in terms of disaffected employees and lost opportunities will be very high indeed.

Having established that the learning log is quintessential to action learning, set members are encouraged throughout the start-up workshop to develop their own individual formats for their logbooks. To help them to start I suggest they might consider using headings based on:

People

Who did I meet this week who made an impact upon me? What was the reason for this impact? What they said? The way they said it? Their mannerisms? The quality of thought? Physique?

What kind of people do I respond well to? Are there personality types to whom I respond negatively? Do I feel that I have made an impact on someone? What caused it? Have I made a negative impression? What did I do wrongly?

Thoughts and ideas

Out of all the thoughts and ideas that I have been exposed to this week (not necessarily as part of the action learning programme), which ones have impressed me? What will I do about them?

Events

Consider all the activities I have been involved in – for example, meetings, courses, interviews, shop-floor crises. What have I learned from each one, both on the spot and after reflection.

How would I modify my actions if a similar event happened in the future?

Planning to learn

Look forward to next week. What learning opportunities do I know are going to arise? What do I expect to learn from them? How will I manage the learning?

Throughout these suggestions I use the word 'feel' as well as the more expected 'think' and 'believe'. The intensely private nature of the learning log takes us into feelings, an area our business and management training has tended to discount and even distance us from. The instruction given to the participants was that each set member should design the format for his or her own logbook. Yet the chances are that the set will come up with one common format. A good omen. They have already absorbed the message that as comrades in adversity they benefit from sharing ideas and working together.

At the close of the session I remind the set that the logbook is a personal and private document. No one else may ever see it. However, as set adviser I am only too willing to discuss the logbook's contents and conclusions.

The learning log is both a means of learning and a record of learning. It is a personal diary and an enforcer of reflecting. Because it is an intensely personal document which is unlikely ever to be published, the format, the style and certainly the content will vary from person to person. Understandably, the hard-headed, practical, down-to-earth manager driven by an over-zealous activist learning style may have difficulties coming to terms with the necessity of keeping a learning log. At the outset he or she may see no value in it at all. By the end of the programme, however, the learning log may have become part of that manager's everyday life.

Worth mentioning, too, is the almost therapeutic function the learning log performs as an instrument for relieving pent-up tensions. The act of writing down thoughts, feelings and impressions becomes a safety valve. This may explain why so many managers caught up in the hurly-burly of corporate life find the learning log so valuable and continue to use it long after the action learning programme is over. The term 'log' evokes the written word: but I have known the learning log be on tape, the learner talking to his or her tape recorder in the car or at other convenient moments.

With professional institutions now demanding proof of members' continuing professional development (CPD), and the Management Charter Initiative (MCI) insisting on personal portfolios as proof of learning, the learning log and its variants are beginning to play an increasingly important role in management education and development.

Alan Mumford[1] has written about the way in which managers declare that they have learnt from experience, and he adds that they have not done very well. Learning from experience is usually a haphazard affair, often only recognized in hindsight. For most people it is unplanned and it is rarely reflected upon, and thus much of the learning potential is lost. What if we were able to plan to learn from experiences we knew we were going to have? Jane Else[2] says:

Most people agree that they learn from experience, but that is an accidental and unconscious process.

There are many advantages of consciously learning from experience, and of expecting to learn from both future and past experiences. For example:

- it helps you to learn from your successes, not just from your mistakes;
- it makes it more likely that you will transfer your learning;
- it can help you plan for future, similar situations; to plan what you will do the same, what you will do differently.

If we look at our diaries or appointment books we shall inevitably see activities which are going to take place during the next few weeks. These could be meetings with suppliers, with customers or clients, or with colleagues.

There may be committee meetings to attend. There may be other meetings in connection with social activities, charity work or our professional institution. A visit to another organization may be scheduled. All of these are learning opportunities: we can plan to learn from them. What we have to do is decide what it is that we want to observe or test.

Alan Mumford lists fourteen skills which are involved in learning effectively. They include being able to:

- identify one's own learning needs;
- plan one's personal learning;
- use learning opportunities;
- review how one learns;
- listen to other people;
- accept help from other people;
- deal with criticism;
- live with risk and ambiguity;
- analyse how successful colleagues behave;
- develop self-awareness;
- communicate freely;
- review what has been learned.

Mumford identifies two types of learners: 'planners' and 'opportunists'. The planners will have planned their careers, looking for, or more likely manufacturing, the right career opportunities. They know where they want to go. Planning comes naturally to them. Opportunists grab opportunities as they arise, but these opportunities have always been created by other people, by circumstance. However, says Mumford, the opportunist is quite capable not only of welcoming these learning opportunities, but also of squeezing the last ounce of learning out of them.

At that start-up workshop the competent set adviser will at least suggest to the opportunist that the skills and approach of the planner are well worth emulating. He or she will also discuss how the skills which we listed above can all be observed, reflected upon and practised within the action learning programme. The learning log captures the set member's immediate reaction to a situation, records the later process of reflection, and notes how the set member intends to behave when he or she is in a similar future situation. The learning log is concerned with 'soft' data: thoughts, feelings, impressions and reactions.

The set adviser will go on to explain how set members can get the most out of set meetings and other set activities. The action learning programme presents the set with a variety of learning opportunities, in most cases learning opportunities that the set itself has called for or created. They review their individual learning processes with each other and with the set adviser. By the very nature of the project work they have to develop their listening skills. As comrades in adversity they learn how to accept help and how to deal with bad news. In pushing forward the project they learn how to take risks and how to live with ambiguity and anxiety.

The set meeting allows the set member to observe these skills in action and analyse the behaviour of his fellows. What makes a colleague effective or ineffective, what makes one person succeed in one situation but fail miserably in another? I upset John – how? How could the situation have been better handled? If I were in a similar situation again, what would I do differently? What have I learnt from this experience? From the very beginning of the start-up workshop and the team effectiveness workshop, the set members have been developing an increased self-awareness. They have also practised the skills of sharing information and working as a team.

The set member's ability to review and bring into focus what he or she has learnt is put to the test when the learning summaries, based upon the learning log, are presented in front of the client, the set and selected guests. This aspect is discussed more fully in Chapter 7.

Working as a team

In Chapter 4 we described the team roles identified by Meredith Belbin. For a project team to succeed there must be an understanding of who is good at what, and how all the skills and abilities within the team can be harnessed and used to best effect. With many teams this understanding develops slowly and haphazardly over a protracted period of time. In action learning we want to help the set to become an effective team as quickly as possible. During the start-up workshop the set can identify some of the elements that go into making a team successful by concentrating on team roles. Later in the programme, after the set has gained some experience of working together, the team effectiveness workshop will take the process further.

My own approach at the start-up workshop is to get the set to complete the Self-Perception Inventory and post the results on to a flipchart, so that they share the information about their preferred roles from the outset. A short session on theory follows. Here the set adviser (or tutor) takes the opportunity to strangle misconceptions at birth. Plants do not spend their working day giving utterance to inspired ideas. Shapers are not always organizing others, hustling them to their own ends. Co-ordinators are not benign co-ordinators all of the time – and so forth. Team roles are sets of behaviours we habitually use when the situation allows us to.

What, then, I ask them to discuss, are the implications for the set? What roles are missing? Is there an over-abundance of other roles? Bearing in mind that most set members will have strengths in two or even three roles, what is the composite picture of the set? What will they have to guard against – too much intellectual debate with not enough action? Too much action without enough thought? Lack of finishing? Not making use of available external resources? In effect, what are the set's weaknesses as a team and how are they going to compensate for them? Plus the converse, of course – what are their strengths, and how are they going to capitalize on them?

The role of the client at the start-up workshop

Having made a substantial contribution during the steps leading up to the start-up workshop, the client now has to take on a new role. He has to influence the set in such a way that the set members retain ownership of the project but are prevented from setting off down unproductive paths.

As the owner of the problem, the client will almost certainly have his or her own views as to what the ideal solution should look like. For most managers this leads to the most difficult aspect of the action learning programme. After all, the argument goes, managers are paid to have answers to problems. However, not only has the client not been able to get an answer himself to this particular problem, he or she must now face the possibility, even the probability, that the set may produce a solution which he, the client, would never have thought of. Furthermore, the client will be expected to be a prime mover in getting the solution implemented. We now see why it is so important that the client really is committed to action learning.

Several years ago I was set adviser to an action learning programme run by a London borough council. There were, in fact, four sub-sets, each with its own client. Before the start-up workshop began the clients asked me for a list of ground rules for clients. I had to admit that there was none that I could immediately lay my hands on, but promised to put a few guidance notes together.

The result was the expected mix of dos and don'ts. Perhaps the strongest advice was that the client should discipline himself to keep his own view of the ultimate solution to himself, no matter how great the temptation to nudge the set down a predetermined path. On the other hand, to guide the set away from a suggested course of action when the client knew that, for political or other reasons, the outcome would be wasted effort, was very much an essential part of the client's job. Fundamental, too, was the client's role as tutor, getting the set to reflect upon their activities by constructive questioning.

One injunction was that clients should beware of setting off on ego trips, something which can happen all too easily even to the most conscientious of clients.

When the client comes to the start-up workshop he or she is only too well aware of the symptoms of the problem, and may even have attempted a written definition of it. The first task of the client, however, is to wait for the set to present their own definition of the problem. This is where debate starts. Not surprisingly, the set's initial definition is almost always significantly different from that of the client. The gap has to be first narrowed and then bridged.

The process of bringing the two definitions closer together is one of mutual questioning and seeking clarification. It is not confrontational. The client asks the set why they see things this way, why they interpret these symptoms that way, what basic assumptions underlie certain other assumptions, and so on. Similarly, the set questions the client's interpretation of the problem. After maybe an hour of discussion the client and the set retire separately to prepare a revised definition of the problem.

Another meeting between client and set. Another period of exploration and discussion. In all likelihood another parting for both client and set to rework their definition.

It is usually at the third meeting that one single definition is agreed upon.

The protracted debate and negotiation to reach one agreed definition ensures two things: firstly, that everybody has an in-depth understanding of the problem, and secondly, that there is a problem definition which can be translated into a project statement.

The process by which the problem is turned into a project

statement is a repeat of the problem definition procedure, except that the client's greater awareness of what is possible and what is not is called into play. When we first discussed aspects of the project in Chapter 1 we said that 'participants [set members] should be challenged and extended without feeling threatened by the prospect of failure, either individually or as a project group'. Many sets will be tempted to set unrealistically ambitious goals for the project. A few may need to be reminded that, with the backing of the client and the commitment of the organization, they can achieve much more than they are proposing.

Eventually client and set agree the project statement, usually expressed in terms such as 'The purpose of this project is to . . .'. At this stage, however, there is no attempt to put a time frame into the statement. That will come later in the start-up workshop, once the set has had a tutorial input on project management and resource allocation. At that stage the client will become involved again, until the project statement is fully defined and qualified.

Tutor, client and set adviser should all stress to the set that the project statement is a starting-point. The project is taking place in real life. In real life the environment is constantly changing. During the life of the project the set and the client may have to restate the project – or even the problem – because of significant changes beyond their control.

Towards the end of the workshop the client will have the opportunity to plan how they should work together. How often will the set meet with the client? For what purposes? Should it be the whole set, or only representatives? What about informal meetings and one-to-one counselling? Just what do the set expect from the client, and the client from the set?

The role of the set adviser at the start-up workshop

Organiser, controller, tutor, counsellor, master of ceremonies – these are just a few of the duties performed by any set adviser during the start-up workshop.

It may be helpful to look at these various facets of set advising under separate headings.

The set adviser as organizer

By the time the start-up workshop arrives the organizing and planning has been completed. For weeks the set adviser has been working towards this event. He or she will have arranged the venue (which on this occasion is likely to be an hotel or conference centre), organized the meeting rooms, and made sure that such necessities as overhead projectors, flipcharts and other equipment are in place and in working order. Very importantly, the figurehead speaker who will open the proceedings will have been briefed, and the tutors who will deliver those parts of the programme that the set adviser will not be conducting will have been engaged and briefed.

All that remains for the set adviser as organizer to do is to oversee the progress of the workshop. The programme should move forward in a planned, logical sequence. If anything goes wrong – if, for example, a tutor fails to appear on cue – everyone will look to the set adviser to put an alternative plan into operation. The set adviser owns the process. He is the only person who can find a way out of a complex situation.

The set adviser as tutor

As the owner of the action learning process, the set adviser will be expected to tutor the set in all aspects of action learning and immediately related subjects, such as learning styles and the use of the learning log.

At the moment, most action learning practitioners have a background in training and development or, sometimes, personnel. It is only natural that they should present the sessions on action learning, learning styles, learning logs, and team effectiveness, leaving the more technical subjects of project design and management to tutors better qualified in that field. Even where the set adviser comes from a discipline other than training and development or personnel, he or she would be expected to lead the core action learning subjects, farming out other sessions.

The set adviser must acquit himself or herself well as a presenter. The start-up workshop will be the first opportunity to appear in this softly authoritative role and to gain the confidence of the set.

The set adviser as counsellor

Right from the word go there will be those who will want guidance and reassurance from the set adviser at an individual level. The set adviser therefore needs to be easily approachable and to have the skills through which to reassure the participant. Listening skills in particular are important.

The good news is that this is a passing phase. Any dependence upon the set adviser will soon be transferred to the set itself once the set becomes a reality and develops a culture of its own. One of the strongest aspects of the culture of action learning sets is the extent to which members support each other. No matter what difficulties or reservations the set member may have, he or she will find positive help within the set.

The set adviser as continuity man or woman

Having masterminded the sequence of events throughout the workshop, the set adviser has finally to make sure that the set and the client go away from the workshop knowing exactly what is to happen next: simple things, like when they are going to meet, how often and at what time. During the session on project management the set looked at resource allocation and drew up a time schedule. The task now is to convert that into dates in the diary.

This is where the set has to look for positive guidance from their set adviser. In planning life after start-up the set will need the kind of information set out below.

The logistics – some considerations

Typically, an in-company action learning programme might consist of, say, twelve formal 'set meetings', each meeting lasting for three to four hours. In many cases these meetings are only partly in company time, and 3 p.m. to 7 p.m. is a common choice. The argument for encroaching on the employee's own time is that the employee stands to benefit from the action learning process. The meetings tend to be fortnightly, or at the rate of three per month, arranged around holidays, month-ends, and the commitments of the set members.

The set meeting normally has three phases: the first part lasts for maybe half an hour, during which members update each other and brief the set adviser. This, in the early stages of the programme, is followed by a tutorial, a talk requested by the set and given by an external or internal expert. The tutorial may take an hour or more and is then followed by a working session during which the set makes use of the skills and knowledge of the tutor to progress the project.

The difficulty is that we cannot foresee all the inputs we may require as the programme develops and opens up new ground for exploration. To be able to cope with this we need two things: blanks scheduled into the programme, and a well-connected set adviser who is quick off the mark and able to procure the services of the right tutor at the right time.

The total time taken for an action learning programme is important. Time taken on the programme is time spent away from the daily routine. Ironically, those managers whose time is already fully committed are the managers who would benefit, and benefit from, the programme. If the time scale is too tight, the day-to-day job will suffer and resentment and frustration may creep in. If it is too extended, disenchantment and a feeling of 'it can't be that important anyway' will appear.

Striking the right balance between the frequency of meetings and the overall time span is essential to a successful outcome.

The shortest action learning programme that I have run lasted fourteen weeks. This was a programme that determined the future of a small graphic design company. The company was in a serious financial position and despite a wealth of talent and a strong order book, was in danger of going under. Time was of the essence. Everybody was involved in every meeting, from the two partners to the receptionist. They worked in two sets. During the meetings a temporary receptionist was called in from an agency to look after the switchboard and take messages. Urgency was paramount. Many of the ideas that flowed from the 3 p.m. to 7 p.m. meetings were implemented next day. Today the company is financially sound and making headway into new markets.

At the other end of the scale one action learning programme took more than eighteen months from start-up to final implementation. However, the action learning part proper (i.e. from start-up to the presentation to the client and his panel) took only the scheduled eight months, but before the recommendations could be implemented they had to be put forward to the trade union at the annual wages round. This took a further ten months.

Most action learning programmes of the type we are discussing (i.e. in-company programmes with all of the set addressing the same issues) last from four to ten months. The only proviso is to take annual holidays into account when scheduling a programme. One that started in June and ran through July, August and September would become rather fragmented, despite every set member having the responsibility of keeping every other member up to date.

Apart from set meetings there are also workshops to be built into the programme. Workshops are a means of developing skills which will be needed in the course of the programme. As skills need to be taught and then practised and polished, workshops usually take one or more days. Unlike meetings, workshops are normally held off site unless the organization boasts adequate training facilities.

Two workshops in particular are predictable and can be planned into the schedule during the start-up workshop: team effectiveness and presentation skills, the latter making extensive use of CCTV.

The venue – a place of one's own?
The venue for set meetings should be as spacious as possible. Whether we are catering for a set of eight, or several sets

working simultaneously, they will need room to spread themselves. There will need to be enough space for one or more flipcharts and an overhead projector. If tutors are to present well, they will have to feel comfortable in their surroundings. Giving a tutorial in cramped surroundings with inadequate equipment can be anything but comfortable.

Action learners invariably produce a staggering amount of paperwork. At the end of the meeting the key items will be retained for future reference and the rest will be scrapped. In the meantime flipchart papers and other material will be spread around the room. Having tables along the walls is one solution. There should also be room (and chairs) for those who are on tap – for instance, the set adviser and the tutor.

The ideal is a room made available for exclusive use by the set, and I have known sets happily trade space for exclusivity. This also has the advantage of increasing further the visibility of the action learning programme when a sign announcing 'Action Learning Room' is displayed on the door.

In conclusion

The start-up workshop is fundamental to the success of the action learning programme. I have known successful programmes grow out of start-up workshops which were no more than adequate, but I have not known or heard of any successful action learning programme developing from a shoddy, ill-prepared and uncommitted start-up.

For this reason we have spent a great deal of time looking at what ideally should go into a start-up workshop for a one-project-per-set (or sub-set) programme. In particular, we have emphasized the learning aspects: self awareness, teamwork and the learning log. We have examined the roles played during the start-up workshop by the client and set adviser, and we have commented upon the administrative arrangements, the logistics.

Flexibility, however, remains the keynote of action learning. This chapter sets out the nature and content of a start-up workshop designed to meet the needs of one type of action learning programme. Many will say that the detail is over-prescriptive, but it is no more than a model, a suggestion. The important thing is that participants and clients leave the workshop having agreed what has to be achieved, and with the knowledge and skills that will allow them to take the first tentative steps.

In Chapter 9 start-up workshops for different types of action learning programmes will be discussed.

References

1   Mumford, A. (1980), *Making Experience Pay*, Maidenhead: McGraw-Hill.
2   Else, J. (1992), 'Learning Logs and Reflection Skills', *Training and Development*, March.

6 Running the programme

The start-up workshop has created an eagerness to get on with the project. The set members now know the nature of the task they have to tackle. They have defined the problem and agreed it with their client and then moved on to restate the problem as a project. They know what help to expect from the client and the role he or she will play throughout the programme.

Set members also know what to expect from the set adviser. They will look to him or her for coaching and guidance, at least in the early days of the programme when they are still unsure of themselves in the new roles that they have acquired. At the outset the set adviser will be the key figure who knows the rules and can mastermind the process. As the set gains confidence the members will begin to take charge of the process and of their own learning: action learning is learner driven, and the set adviser is there to be used by the set.

From being the source of knowledge and know-how, the set adviser will soon become the oiler of wheels, the procurer of tutors, the supplier of contacts, and eventually, the odd jobber. One difficulty which many set advisers experience is letting go.

This is particularly so for many who have been trained as 'facilitators' and feel the need to make a continuing contribution long after the set has assumed responsibility for its own learning. Humility can be a great asset for the set adviser.

Action learning cannot be planned in fine detail at the outset. Action learning is learner driven and deals with real life situations in the here-and-now. Things change: goalposts move, quite legitimately, as fresh information surfaces. At the start-up workshop the set planned, with guidance from the set adviser, what tutorials the set would need. Most were predictable. After all, action learning is about change, therefore we need to know how to manage change. We also need to know how to think creatively. Action learning is teamwork, and so we need to know how to work effectively as a team.

In an action learning programme a lull often sets in at about the halfway stage. By this time information has been pulled in from a variety of sources, ideas have been mooted, discussed and rejected, and, rather than diminishing, the problem seems to become bigger and bigger. This happens after the initial weeks of tutorial-type set meetings. Once the set moves into the action research phase and from there into consolidating data and generating alternative solutions, the impetus picks up again. The mid-life crisis is over.

A model for reference

Action learning programmes come in many formats, but as we are considering specifically in-company programmes (as opposed, for example, to those which form part of a business school qualification course, or are run on a consortium basis), the case outlined below, based on a real-life action learning programme, serves as a model for reference.

The company concerned employs 1000 people. They design, manufacture and sell photographic materials to industry and the public sector. Over the last 18 months their market share has been eroded. From being the market leader, the company is now third or fourth in the league table. A new entrant has entered the market, backed by its diversifying, multi-national parent. A UK-based international company, which had always been a competitor but had been content with a small market share for what it regarded as a 'sideline' to its main activities, is becoming increasingly aggressive.

A smaller competitor has just introduced a new product range which is having an impact on the public sector market: and, of course, market size has diminished while manufacturing and distribution costs have risen.

Faced with this state of affairs, eight people have been selected to form an action learning set. Their task is to examine the situation and produce a recommended plan of action to enable the company to increase its profitability and regain its market share. There is an explicit agreement that their recommendations will be implemented, so the choice of client is critical.

The set members are:

The marketing manager
A regional sales manager
The manufacturing director
The deputy accountant
The personnel officer
A major account executive
An information systems officer
A research and development chemist.

The selection has been on the basis of knowledge plus need: all have a contribution to make by virtue of the jobs they are doing, and all will have an opportunity for growth and development, from their exposure to one another and to new concepts and methods.

Notably, the manufacturing director is the only board member, the sales and marketing director preferring to help from the sidelines. A powerful and didactic individualist, he felt that others might defer to him in discussions and that his presence might therefore be counterproductive.

Altogether, three levels of hierarchy are represented. The

information systems officer and the R & D chemist, apart from being able to make immediate contributions, have already been earmarked for wider responsibilities. The managing director has recognized that participation in the action learning programme is an ideal vehicle for giving everybody involved a wider perspective and a deeper understanding of the industry, the company and the business.

The client is the managing director. At first the managing director wanted to be a set member. This meant that he would have had to ask his own supervisor at group level to be the client, but this presented geographical and other difficulties. For a while he thought about being both client and set member, a practice which, although not common, has worked successfully in smaller organizations. A main factor in his decision not to be a set member was that he did not want to inhibit the contribution of the more junior members.

As this is the company's first action learning programme, they have enlisted the help of an external consultant with experience of running in-house action learning programmes. The consultant has been involved from the early discussions onwards. He recognizes that by the very nature of the action learning process, if he does his job as set adviser well, the next action learning programme will need minimal, if any, outside assistance.

Out of the start-up workshop came the schedule shown in Figure 6.1. It is typical of many in-house, one-project-per-set (or per sub-set) action learning programmes which have been run in the public sector as well as in private companies.

Collecting data – the tutorials

At the start-up workshop the set decided what tutorial inputs they would want during the first few meetings. As a meeting only lasts three to four hours, including the preliminary discussion and updating, it is important for the set to plan the meeting and then control it.

Between 30 and 45 minutes is usually sufficient for the set

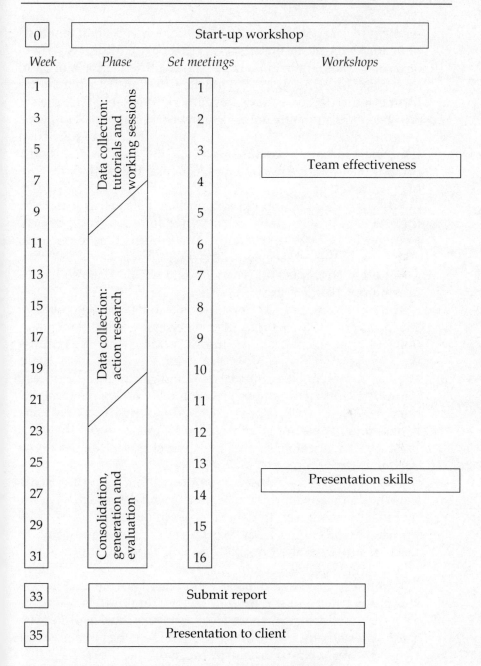

Figure 6.1 Plan of a typical action learning programme

members to report back to each other on the activities they
have undertaken since the last meeting. If the tutor has arrived
before the meeting begins, it may be worthwhile for him to sit
on the sidelines, getting a feel for the situation. This is a matter
for the set to decide. There is usually no problem at all: the set
has been through the initial stages of getting to know one
another during the start-up workshop. Having established
tentative working relationships they now want to start the
programme, and are not likely to feel inhibited by the presence
of a stranger.

Whether or not to appoint a chairperson is again a matter for
the set, and may depend on company culture, personal
preferences or mere expediency. The introduction to personal
styles which the set received at the start-up workshop will have
given them concepts and personal data which will also have a
bearing on this decision.

The appointment of a 'librarian' is a must. In the course of
the programme a plethora of paperwork will be generated.
Some of it will come from the tutorials, some from the ensuing
working sessions, some from the action research, and what is
needed is someone to pounce upon and retain every flipchart,
hand-out, cutting or other piece of relevant (or conceivably
relevant) paperwork. Three months and two days into the
programme, some set member is going to ask to see the chart
produced by speaker so-and-so when she was talking about
such-and-such.

One thing the set adviser must do without fail is to ensure
that the tutor is well briefed, either by himself or, preferably,
by one or more set members. The tutor must arrive well
prepared to talk about what the set needs to know and wants to
discuss, not what the tutor likes to talk about. This holds true
whether the tutor is an internal specialist or an external one.

A refinery accountant once complained to me that it had
taken him three days to prepare a 90-minute session on
refinery accounting practices to give to an action learning set.
Then, after talking to one of the set members, he spent another
two days reshaping his talk to meet the set's exact requirements.

External tutors should be well versed in action learning and accustomed to working in the learner-driven mode. Unfortunately not many tutors are. On several occasions I have asked potential tutors if they knew about action learning and have been assured that, yes, they knew all about it. When I probed more deeply it soon became apparent that they, like many others, were simply bemused by the number of training fads and techniques which had built the word *action* into their title. The growth of outward-bound-type management courses, with their implied *activity*, had added to the confusion.

The right tutor, then, may be difficult to find. Often it is a case of balancing professional credibility against the ability to reach a rapport with the set and present well. The tutor must also be willing to become embroiled in the working session which follows on from his presentation. Many a set has been let down by tutors who have arrived to give a potted version of their 'standard' half-day presentation and then baulked at the idea of becoming involved (and maybe exposed) in the working session.

A point worth considering is that organizations undertake action learning programmes to gain a competitive edge over their rivals. To do this effectively may mean gaining access to the latest concepts and techniques, or even to developments which are still embryonic or at best in the experimental stage. This is where the well-connected set adviser is essential.

Set meetings which consist of tutorial inputs followed by working sessions are the norm for the first few weeks of the action learning programme. This is the period when participants update themselves by building on P (the programmed knowledge of $L = P + Q$), although it is often difficult to differentiate between P and Q (the ability to move forward by posing the apposite question).

These first weeks form the period during which the set, in team development terminology, completes the transition from 'forming' where members are polite, guarded and watchful, through 'storming', the process of adjusting to each other, to 'norming', where skills are developed, procedures established and issues confronted. The next step is to help them move round the team development wheel to 'performing', where members are open, resourceful, flexible and supportive towards each another. To do this we use the team effectiveness workshop.

The team effectiveness workshop

The importance of working effectively as a team was recognized in the start-up workshop when some preliminary work was done, using Belbin's Self-Perception Inventory to identify the personal styles of each set member. Now that the members know each other better in a work situation, it is an appropriate time to run the team effectiveness workshop.

The purpose of the team effectiveness workshop is to help set members understand what makes a team perform well, and then to assist them in applying the principles to their own situation. What strengths and attributes does each member bring to the set? What are the set's overall strengths . . . and weaknesses? Where are the blind spots? How can the set compensate for these blind spots which could well impede performance? How is everything going to be linked together to make sure that nothing falls between the cracks?

As a result of the team effectiveness workshop people start to listen to each other in earnest. Minor so-called personality clashes disappear (cause and effect?), more purposeful use is made of the work preferences within the set, and measures are taken to safeguard the set from potential disasters. The set is conscious of the need to be creative, to assess and develop ideas, to organize its resources and meet its deadlines, to monitor the quality of its output, to make the best use of outside resources, and to keep other parts of the organization up to date with what the set is doing.

In addition to using the new skills and understanding to improve the performance of the action learning set, each member carries the newly found skills and confidence back into his or her daily work.

Having reached this point in the action learning programme the set will be getting ready to move away from tutorial-type meetings and become involved in action research. This does not mean an end to tutorials, it is simply that they will probably need to use more time debating the results of their research. Indeed, it is during the action research phase that the demand for unpredicted tutorials is most likely to arise.

The team effectiveness workshop is described in more detail in Appendix 3.

Collecting data – action research

To many people the term 'research' conjures up scenes of detailed academic experimentation followed by endless sifting and collation of information. Not so in action research.

Action research is undertaken to bring about change. In traditional research the researcher's preoccupation is with establishing the 'truth' of a hypothesis. The research findings are then handed over to those who will take action based on these findings. Here the researcher is not the change agent. Roger Bennett and Jim Oliver describe traditional research as 'arm's-length research' and action research as 'arm-in-arm research'.[1] In the latter case all the set are involved in carrying out research into an immediate problem, and all have a vested interest in implementing the results.

The need for action research becomes apparent to the set after the first four or five set meetings. They have listened to and worked with the tutors. Having focused in on aspects of the problem they recognize as critical, they find themselves in need of more information, but this time information that is in the form of views, opinions, experiences. So the action learning questions begin:

- Who knows about this type of problem?
- Who has been in a similar situation?
- What did they do about it?
- What mistakes did they make?
- Who is a good example of 'best practice'?
- Whose brains can we pick?

These are the kinds of questions which arise. More often than not the answers lie outside the set's own organization. Ideally we should be collecting data on the same subject from a variety of sources and in significant volume, otherwise we may end up with data that does no more than verify the set's opinions.

The steps in action research within an action learning programme are:

- agreeing what information is required;
- deciding how the information is to be collected;
- planning how to feed the data back to the set;
- collecting the data;
- debating and agreeing the conclusions from the data;
- planning action.

Among the methods of data collection which are most commonly used in action research are:

- questionnaire-based surveys;
- interview-based surveys;
- fact-finding visits to other organizations.

Each method of data collection has its full share of advantages and disadvantages. It is essential to consider the length of time any chosen method will take, the availability of materials, the complexity of the process, and, inevitably, the cost. It may be that all these considerations are secondary to having accurate and totally reliable information, but in most action research instances a less than rigorous approach will suffice.

Central to the action research phase is the set adviser. If the set adviser is an experienced external 'well-connected' consultant he will be able to use his own network to gain access to other organizations. An internal set adviser will also have his or her own network, and this network will expand quickly in the course of running action learning programmes. Companies which use action learning like to share their experiences and their contacts with others, either through organizations such as the UK-based International Foundation for Action Learning (IFAL), or through personal contacts.

This period of the project can become administratively

messy. With some sub-groups going off to other companies to discuss common problems and how they were tackled, and other groups working in other areas of action research, the set adviser may become, for a time, the only person who has anything like a clear picture of what is happening between set meetings.

Action research is an exciting, revealing activity within the action learning process. The somewhat threatening (or at least mystifying) title 'action research' should not deter anyone from engaging in action learning.

Action research examples

Surveys: by questionnaire

It was the fifth set meeting of an action learning set. The company was a motor vehicle importer and distributor, and the action learning programme concerned itself with several issues in the Parts Distribution Centre. One major issue which the set was tackling was the payment system in operation in the warehouse. The warehouse despatched spare parts to all the dealers in the UK.

Sales of these imported vehicles had increased year by year and, consequently, so had the demand for spare parts. The number of 'lines' had also increased as new models were introduced.

The emphasis had always been on getting parts out to dealers as quickly as possible. The warehouse staff had coped, but wages had risen to an unacceptably high level. Although the company had a loyal workforce committed to the business, there were severe disadvantages: for example, recruitment was minimal because no one left except through retirement, there was muted resistance to the introduction of new technology, and volume throughput took precedence over quality of service.

It was against this backdrop that the action learning set, composed of seven senior and middle managers, was discussing what kind of remuneration system should replace the existing one. The choices were reduced to straight salary, salary plus bonus, or salary plus bonus plus benefits. Eventually the debate narrowed down to what the split should be between salary and bonus, and what benefits the workforce would want. Straight salary? Salary plus small bonus? A 50:50 split? What about benefits – changes to the car leasing scheme (available to all established employees)? Private medical insurance?

After some time in lively discussion one set member stated, 'We know that what they really want is . . .'. Silence. Then a quiet voice said, 'How on earth do *we* know what *they* want?'

In action learning, pronouncements made in the heat of debate often lead on to greater things. Here the questioner had challenged an assumption, and out of that came agreement that objective information on what the warehouse workforce wanted in terms of their remuneration package could only come from the warehouse employees themselves.

The resulting survey lasted seven weeks. Time constraints (the annual wages round was only a few months away) meant that the survey would have to be completed as soon as possible. 'Acceptability' in terms of impartiality and confidentiality meant that the set could not carry out the survey themselves, even had they had the time to do so.

A market research consultant was brought in. She had worked with action learning sets before and knew that she would have to work hand in hand with the set throughout the design and implementation of the survey. This would call for a far greater degree of contact with the client (the set) than would be expected on a normal assignment. She not only had to get results, she had to pass on some of her expertise in the process.

The trade union representatives were invited to have one of their members join the set for these discussions. They declined and remained uninterested during the initial stages. Later they adopted a neutral stance before eventually becoming positive and supportive, thanks largely to good communication and an open flow of information.

The data from the survey proved crucial to the ultimate success of the project.

The way in which the survey was designed and managed illustrates some key aspects of conducting this type of survey:

- everybody on site must know what is going on, not just those who are immediately involved;
- those who are to be involved must be adequately briefed, preferably in small groups, and given the opportunity to ask questions;
- confidentiality must be guaranteed;
- interim and final feedback sessions to the set must be properly planned;
- respondents must receive feedback from the researcher, in small groups and with the opportunity to ask questions;
- Learning must not be ousted by task.

Survey: by interviews
In the case above, the questionnaire-based survey was supplemented by a series of one-to-one interviews to probe in more depth the issues being explored. These interviews were limited to 30 per cent of the respondents, representing a cross-section and based on criteria laid down by the researcher. The interviews were conducted by trained staff brought in by the consultant. Thirty minutes was allowed for each interview.

Very different was the action research undertaken by the staff of a small graphic design company. This company had started life as two separate but neighbouring companies, operating in the same field and frequently subcontracting work to each other. In due course both realized that there were significant benefits to be gained from amalgamating, and this they did. The result was a company with twelve employees, including the two partners.

Action learning was brought in when the company found itself in a life and death situation. On the plus side there was an immense pool of talent and enthusiasm, a well-filled order book, and several large contracts in the offing. On the minus side were low profitability, poor-quality output and haphazard client service.

The tutorial inputs which had formed the early data collection phase had been team effectiveness (as a one-day workshop), client care, creative thinking, paper management and managing change. The two sets had already implemented several of the ideas which had been developed during these tutorials and the following working sessions. One big problem nevertheless remained: despite their acceptance and use of client care concepts, they felt that very little had changed. In their own words, how could they improve the quality of creativity and customer care? Answer: they had to go and ask their customers.

Between them the sets arranged to interview 20 clients, ranging from major accounts to small ones. The interviewers used a list of prepared questions to cover what they saw as main areas worth pursuing, before opening the discussion up.

When they came to analyse the results they found that the answers to the prepared questions merely confirmed what they already knew. It was the data which came from the open-ended discussion in response to questions like 'What should we be doing that we don't do now?' or 'What would you do if you were us?' which made them drastically change the way they delivered after-sales service.

The last two decades have seen sweeping changes in local government, causing local authorities to face a series of new issues and rethink strategies. Many have made profitable use of action learning. One large London borough council used action learning to plan and implement change in several areas, including privatization of services and public relations. The set confronting the public relations issue carried out a survey by questionnaire to test the public's perception of the role and effectiveness of the council, and to gather suggestions as to how the council might offer a better service.

The survey was followed up with interviews with a cross-section of the community. Again, it was the interviews which gave the key insights into what was really needed to improve the image and services of the council.

On the privatization project, the question facing the set (a different set from the one tackling public relations) was the extent to which privatization was feasible in terms of cost benefit, public reaction and employee relations, and how to go about the process of privatizing.

No questionnaire survey on this occasion, just visits to local authorities which had already successfully privatized many of their services, and interviews with those officers who had been involved in the planning and implementation stages. One question in particular yielded seminal results: 'If you were to do all over again, what would you do differently?'

Group interviews can provide a wealth of information and opinion in a relatively short time. Numbers should be limited to eight, and the time to an hour. A certain amount of scene-setting is necessary to put people at their ease. Once under way, the interaction between the members of the group can elicit much more information than is usual in a one-to-one situation – the main difficulty is capturing it all.

This technique worked well with groups of refinery maintenance supervisors who might have been less forthcoming had they been asked to take part in more formal one-to-one interviews.

Fact-finding visits
Visits to other organizations to see, as well as to discuss, how others have overcome problems similar to your own are invaluable. Carrying out surveys and conducting interviews can be lonely affairs, but fact-finding visits to other organizations are usually undertaken by several people or even the whole set. There is often an air of expectancy, if not excitement. The mood is one of 'We know the direction we're going in, we've heard what the tutors have had to say, now let's see for ourselves how these people have tackled it and see what we can learn from them.'

Visits normally give the set the opportunity to talk to people as the opportunity arises; looking at systems or machines, for example, it is possible to get the operators' views as well as those of the supervisors and managers.

It is unlikely that a set will be able to visit a competitor to gain from the competitor's experience. More likely, visits will be to organizations which have had problems similar to the one you are working on, and have successfully overcome them. It may be that they are now regarded as 'centres of excellence' or custodians of 'best practice' in this particular field.

During one action learning programme a computer company, supplying self-employed IT and IS specialists to clients on a contract basis, needed to overhaul its personnel records system. In the course of its action research it arranged to visit a secretarial agency which, after much research of its own, had recently installed a state-of-the-art system designed to take them into the next decade. The common factor was that both organizations had to maintain and continuously update records on a large number of mobile people who only occasionally worked for them.

In another action learning programme a professional partnership in Britain wanted to explore the feasibility of setting up branches in continental Europe. They went to talk to a firm of architects and to a consulting engineering practice. Both had established offices in Europe within the preceding five years. Size and the 'professional' nature of their work was the common factor.

Competitors should not be ruled out altogether – in many industries, sharing information is the norm. In the oil industry competition takes place at the petrol pump: downstream from there a considerable amount of information is exchanged, most of it so far removed from the petrol pump that it can be discussed freely at the various meetings of specialists and industry representatives.

Quid pro quo can apply. The vehicle importing company we have already cited ran a later action learning programme at a different plant, the plant where the vehicles enter the UK, have any transit damage put right, and undergo a pre-delivery inspection before being sent to the dealer. The set knew that one of the problems facing them had already been successfully dealt with by another vehicle importer, a direct competitor.

The set adviser was able to put the set in touch with a senior manager from the other company who, in turn, arranged for the set to visit the plant and inspect the operation they were interested in. He also set up meetings with the engineers and designers who had been involved in the planning and implementation aspects, and they explained in great detail what problems had been met and how they had been overcome.

All the competitor wanted in return was an invitation to visit the set's plant in order to look at some new equipment that had recently been installed and discuss its performance.

Both plants were a long way from their dealers' showrooms.

Consolidating, generating and evaluating

Consolidating really starts when the pressures of time combine with the sheer mass of the data collected to suggest that the time has come to start pulling everything together.

Ideas and opinions have been exchanged and developed ever since the first day of the start-up workshop. Tutors have come in, spoken, shared in the working sessions, and gone. Surveys, whether by questionnaire or interview or both, have added to the stockpile of data, and fact-finding visits have thrown up more ideas and suggested new avenues for research. By this time it is more than likely that diminishing returns will have set in.

The time has come to slow down on the data collection and to start assembling what has already been amassed.

There are several ways in which the activities and energies of the set can be refocused, and all can be planned into the programme during the start-up workshop. The first and obvious way is to have a set meeting (or meetings) where the only item on the agenda is a review of where the set has got to. This is enforced reflection.

For several weeks set members have been pursuing different lines of enquiry, often working individually on specific aspects of the project. Set meetings have been taken up with members reporting back to one another on the general progress of their separate researches and activities. To hold a meeting which, properly handled by the set adviser, addresses questions like:

- where are we now?
- where should we be?
- where do we go from here?
- do we need to reschedule?
- do we need to restate the project?

tends to restore a strong sense of direction, even urgency.

A second refocusing agent is the need at this stage to report back to the client on the progress of the project. There has been intermittent contact with the client during the action research period, but this is a formal meeting between the client and the whole set. In addition to bringing the client completely up to date with the progress of the project, this meeting allows the set to check that they are not going down any blind alleys or into any politically sensitive areas. It also allows the client to brief the set on any matters that might impact upon the project, and satisfy himself that the set is moving towards *implementable* solutions.

A third method of concentrating the collective mind is the presentation skills workshop. This workshop serves three purposes: it develops the presentation skills of each member of the set, it gives confidence to those who would not normally have to speak formally in front of an audience, and it forces the set to think through the shape and content of the formal presentation they will be giving in front of the client and his panel.

In addition to teaching how to plan and deliver a presentation, the presentation skills workshop develops the skills of the participants by getting each one to make a presentation. This is then critically discussed by the other set members as well as by the tutor. The presentation is reworked, represented, and discussed again . . . and again. As all the presentations are based on project material, at the end of the workshop there is a 'draft' version of the presentation proper. The set has a clear impression of what the final result will look like, and of what still remains to be done.

'Creative thinking' is a tutorial which many sets plan into their schedule at the outset, usually slotting it into the first few weeks of the programme. If there has been no creative thinking tutorial, now is an ideal time to introduce one, for the task in front of the set is to generate a range of solutions to the problem they are facing. The tutorial centres around brainstorming techniques and the importance of separating the 'generation' of ideas from the 'evaluation' of these ideas. Once the set gets locked into the detailed evaluation of one idea, the production and development of new ideas stops.

So far we have not singled out any one course of action as the only, or best, one to pursue. In the first place, the presence of options causes debate, and it is earnest debate which safeguards the quality of the final decision by ensuring that all the main aspects have been explored. Secondly, and in action learning equally importantly, it is in debate and discussion, followed by reflection, that learning takes place.

Inevitably the time comes when the set has to submit to the client a fully developed and detailed project report, advocating a plan of action. After the client and other interested parties have had an opportunity to study the report, the set will answer questions and expand upon the report during the formal presentation to the client and the panel.

Figure 6.2 shows in simplified form the sequence of events undertaken by the set in the course of an action learning programme. The sequence starts after the start-up workshop has been completed: the problem and the project statement have been agreed with the client. The starting-point is data collection. As information comes in it is reflected upon and analysed. As the data grows there comes a point when general patterns emerge through synthesis. The set's next activity is to generate possible courses of action based on the available data, and then evaluate these options. Eventually one set of recommendations is put forward to the client for implementation. Notice that implementing the recommendations does not close the loop: it could, in fact, start a new one.

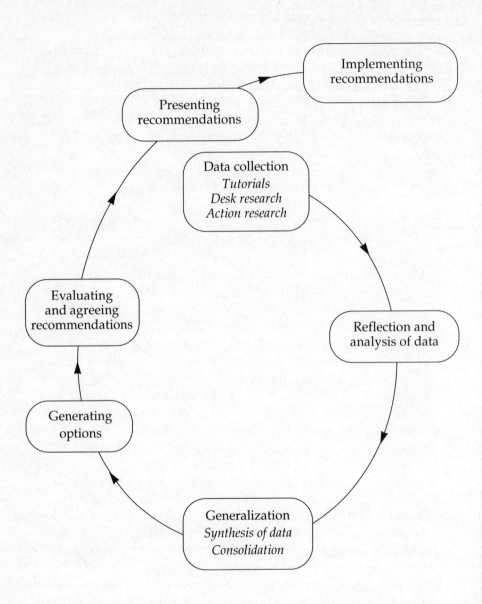

Figure 6.2   The action learning sequence

Reference

1 Bennett, R. and Oliver, J. (1988), *How to Get the Best from Action Research – a Guidebook*, Bradford: MCB–University Press.

7   Presenting the results

The written report

The purpose of the report

People generally write reports for one reason only: they want to make their ideas clear to the reader and, usually, provoke action. One dictionary definition of 'report' is an 'account given or opinion formally expressed after investigation or consideration or collation of information'. This would seem to cover our action learning situation.

In action learning, however, the purpose of the report is far more than that of merely setting out the considered recommendations of the set. In doing this, the report not only has to give the rationale behind these recommendations, it also has to discuss the main ideas which were seriously considered before being rejected. In Chapter 4 we saw how an action learning project had to be complex enough to suggest several possible solutions, each offering scope for debate. From the debate and discussion over the merits of the various alternatives come reflection and learning.

At one level the action learning report presents the set's recommendations, explains why these are being put forward, highlights the also-rans and why they were finally rejected, and becomes a reference point in a quickly changing world.

Our action learning written report has two other purposes. First, the process of having to assemble a report focuses the set's mind and sharpens its thinking. Second, the need for the set to submit a report that will do them justice invariably means that they will have to polish up their report-writing skills.

The report-writing skills that each set member already has will vary from set to set and within each set. A set composed of managers and technical experts may be expected to have a higher order of report-writing skills than one consisting mainly of foremen production supervisors. Nevertheless my experience suggests that both groups need and benefit from the opportunity to examine their business report-writing skills objectively.

The ideal answer is a one-day report-writing workshop, although a tutorial built into a set meeting and followed by practical work on the design of the final report can achieve much in terms of individual and group development. The one-day workshop was particularly effective in one organization where highly technical reports were produced in great numbers. As one of the benefits for the company the set compiled a set of guidelines for the writing of technical reports. They worked. The reports became readable and thus understandable.

The report-writing workshop

The report-writing workshop is designed to enhance the report-writing skills of the set members and to provide a framework around which reports can be assembled.

The timing of the report-writing workshop is critical. If the workshop is held too early in the programme it lacks immediacy – getting down to writing the report is something which can be put off until some future date in the relatively distant future. In the meantime there are other things to get on with, such as data collection and action research visits to other organizations to learn from their experience of similar problems.

Probably the best time to hold a report-writing workshop is when the set has completed its action research and is well into the evaluation stage. This would be round about week 27 on the schedule shown in Figure 6.1. Information has been collected (some of it from tutorials and workshops, some from action research) and has been sifted and appraised. Tentative solutions have been generated. A preliminary evaluation may have resulted in selected proposals being carried forward to the next stage. The end of the project is in sight. Activist and pragmatist learning styles come into their own. There is a real task to be completed and the outcome will be used in the immediate future.

There are two difficulties which the set has to face: how to present their proposals in a sequence that the reader can follow and understand, and how to do so in language that is clear and unambiguous.

One approach to the report-writing workshop is to examine report-writing skills under the headings of 'organization' and 'clarity'. Organization is the starting-point. Many hours of work will already have been put into the project. Ideas will abound. There will be vaguely felt impressions of what the final report should look like. As yet nobody will have made a start on the report. Enter the tutor who is not directly involved in the project and can therefore combine objectivity with report-writing know-how.

One approach which works well is to start the workshop by looking at how reports are organized. My own preference for action learning reports is to use the sequence:

- Title
- Summary
- Introduction
- Recommendations
- Discussion (rationale)
- Appendices.

The summary introduces the recommendations which are later spelt out in greater detail under their own heading.

The set move straight into working on the first outline of the summary. By tackling the summary first they can find that the conclusions they have reached become more sharply defined. This will enable the set to move more easily into evaluating the competing proposals and writing up their recommendations. The supporting discussion, the rationale, will follow naturally, as will the appendices. Frequently the introduction is the last part to be written, and by then there are new insights into why the action learning programme was started in the first place.

By the end of the workshop the set will have a skeleton report prepared. There will be many blanks to be filled in, and much of what they have written will be drastically altered before the report is finalized. However by getting to grips with the report all the preceding work will have been pulled into perspective. Gaps, in terms of what still has to be done, will become clear. Priorities will line themselves up. The pace will quicken.

The workshop will also stress clarity. For many there are two English languages, the spoken and the written. In the report-writing workshop the emphasis is upon bringing the written language closer to the spoken one. This means encouraging the use of everyday words instead of 'learned' ones, and the use of short sentences and short paragraphs. It also means preferring the active voice to the passive and the conversational style to the literary.

The Gunning Fog Index can be introduced as one way of accurately testing the readability of a document. The Index relates the length of sentences in a text to the difficulty of the vocabulary in order to provide a measure of how easy a piece of text is to understand. Gunning held that unwieldy, complicated writing 'fogged up' the ideas. The Index measures the degree of fogging.

Writing which has a high fog index saps the reader's energy, leaving less energy available for comprehension. Ironically, the more difficult an idea is to understand, the simpler should be the language in which it is expressed.

To calculate the fog index, take any piece of text over 100 words in length. The passage must start at the beginning of a sentence, and finish at the end of a sentence. Then:

1   Find the average number of words per sentence. Count *all* the words, even the single letter ones. Count numbers as one word, regardless of the number of digits – 6 is one word, and so is 66,699.235.

2   Total the words of three or more syllables in the complete passage, but do not include:
   i)   proper names, e.g. names of people, companies, products, places;
   ii) compound words made from two or more easily recognizable short words, e.g. narrowboat, horse-power, nevertheless, ghettoblaster;
   iii) verbs which have become three-syllable words through the addition of an -ing or -ed ending.

3   Express the number of words of three or more syllables as a percentage of the total number of words in the passage.

4   Add together the numbers obtained in steps 1 and 2, and multiply the result by 0.4. The result is the fog index for the passage.

The calculations for a readable and understandable piece of business writing might look like:

Total words in selected passage	196
number of sentences	12
average number of words per sentence	16
words of three or more syllables	29
29 as percentage of 196	15
Therefore fog index = (16 + 15) × 0.4	12

The fog index level to aim for in business documents is between 10 and 14. If the level falls below 10 the result may be construed as simplistic or even patronizing. Above 14 the document becomes heavy going and hard work. Where sophisticated technical vocabulary has to be used, the fog index can show where the deadening effect of polysyllabics may be offset by the judicious use of short sentences.

The presentation

Several years after the refinery action learning programme (discussed in Chapter 1) had been completed I returned to the refinery to help with a different aspect of management development. During my two-day visit I met most of the foremen and supervisors who had been set members. Long conversations revealed the extent to which they had been able to make use of the skills they had acquired during the programme. Of the many skills and techniques that were mentioned, two in particular stood out as having made a significant difference to their ability to influence other people. The first of these was the simple concept of psychological stroking. The second was how their ability to influence others, whether superiors, peers or subordinates, had increased dramatically as a result of new-found skills in organizing and presenting information.

At work the first aspect, psychological stroking, is all about giving recognition for a job well done (or badly done). It is the self-imposed discipline of telling colleagues or subordinates that you recognize that they have performed well when they have, or that they have not performed well whenever this is the case. The latter is preferable to saying nothing at all. The introduction to stroking came from the set adviser because it made sense within the context of a discussion on motivation. This digression from our main theme of presentations illustrates how straightforward, easy-to-apply techniques can surface unexpectedly during a set meeting, and have long-lasting benefits.

To return to presentations, the foremen and supervisors recognized that the skills which they used so effectively to organize information and present it to others came directly as a result of the presentation skills workshop they had had to go through in preparing to give the formal presentation to the client and his guests. The refinery set have not been the only ones to comment on the long-term value of the presentation skills workshop. Nor does the 'level' of the set seem to make much difference. First-line managers will be enthusiastic about their new skills and abilities: senior managers will admit to having benefited from having their existing presentation skills updated.

The purpose of the presentation
The final presentation takes place some two to three weeks after the written report has been published. The presentation is normally made to the client and his or her guests. These guests usually include the client's manager, the sponsor, the chief executive, and those managers who have been involved in the project or will be affected directly by the recommendations. This 'panel' will probably number up to ten people. The presentation of each project is usually scheduled to take some 40 minutes, with ample time left for questions and answers.

The overt purpose of the presentation is:

• to expand upon selected aspects of the report;
• to explain in more depth how certain decisions were arrived at;
• to answer questions from the panel.

There is a second order of objectives, however:

• to give set members exposure to more senior management;
• to give meaningful experience in delivering a presentation;
• to increase set members' confidence.

Most of us have a natural apprehension, even fear, of speaking in public. Bad enough when the listeners are friends or colleagues, but much, much worse when the audience is one which can influence our careers! The penalties of failure may appear inordinately high.

In the rare ideal situation all the set members will share

equally in the presentation. However, difficulties can arise on two fronts. There may be a senior person in the set who regularly makes presentations and who, for a variety of reasons, may want to take on a large part of the presenting.

At the other end of the scale may be a set member who is genuinely frightened by the whole prospect, and resists all efforts to persuade and cajole him or her into taking an active part in the presentation. This rarely happens, but when it does the set is likely to be understanding and supportive and will devise their own means of allowing the set member not to present, while at the same time making sure that he or she is fully identified with the presentation.

It is worth stressing that the presentation the set gives to the panel is not a sales presentation in the sense of a win-lose situation. There is no sale to be made. Even before the start of the action learning programme there was an explicit contract that the recommendations developed by the set would be implemented, barring exceptional circumstances outside the immediate control of the organization. From the beginning the client has had the duty of monitoring the progress of the project and making sure that the set did not invest effort in developing solutions that, for political or any other reasons, were not going to be viable. The constant dialogue between client and set has ensured that the recommendations will be implemented.

The presentation does not necessarily stop at the 'final' presentation to the client and his or her guests. In large organizations a well-prepared and delivered presentation can go on tour, communicating the success of the action learning programme to other parts of the organization and creating a heightened interest in possible further uses for action learning. Sometimes the presentation is put on to a professionally produced videotape and copies distributed round the organiz- ation. They are shown with varying degrees of formality. Generally, the tape is introduced by a senior manager at a formal presentation and then played regularly in such places as the cafeteria and the reception area.

The final presentation is often criticized (but not by set

members) for taking up time and energy after the event (the 'event' being the publication of the project's recommendations). Those who put forward this view may have missed the whole ethos of action learning. The presentation marks the culmination of months of hard work, much of it in the set member's own personal time. It demands the acquisition of new skills. It creates confidence. It fulfils the organization's commitment to communicate. More than anything else, it demonstrates that the organization is changing its way of doing things. Organizational development is actually happening.

The presentation skills workshop

The fears and apprehensions of the set members tend to evaporate, or at least diminish, during the course of the presentation skills workshop. The workshop itself is usually typical of its genre. Theoretical inputs are kept to a minimum, with the participants being asked to consider four main aspects of speaking to small groups:

- personal attributes
- the structure of the talk
- the use of visual and other aids
- dealing with questions.

Under personal attributes we are looking at a wide range of factors which includes mannerisms, the use of the voice, eye contact and even posture. Mannerisms are part of our personality, and most of them work for us. Our concern in the presentation skills workshop is to identify those mannerisms which work against us, which the audience finds distracting, and avoid them. The voice is a powerful tool: by varying the pitch and the speed of our delivery we can use the voice to keep the audience interested. Our eyes are our main means of keeping in touch with our listeners. Eye contact is critically important, and for this reason it is stressed and practised throughout the workshop.

Structuring a presentation correctly is of paramount importance. There is a fundamental difference between the structure of a verbal presentation and that of a written report. In the latter the reader can always flip back a few pages to remind himself or herself of the gist of an argument, or to check some statistics. The listener cannot do this, therefore the speaker must regularly reiterate the key messages which have to be put across. As in the old adage, the presenter must tell the listeners what they are going to hear, then let them hear it, and then conclude by telling them what it was that they heard. In the verbal presentation the speaker has control, provided he or has the skill to keep it and exploit it.

The structure also takes into account the need to give the listener a reason for listening, and the need to keep the listener interested all the way through to the conclusion.

When it comes to considering the use of visual aids the message is very clear: Murphy always wins – anything that can go wrong will go wrong. Avoid sophisticated technology – and we might even include the 35mm slide projector in this category. Both the overhead projector (OHP) and the humble flipchart are versatile, easy to master and relatively gremlin-free. Nearly all presentations can be built around the use of these two aids.

The presentation skills workshop gives the set members ample opportunity to practise using the OHP and the flipchart. It also deals with making basic visual aids. Emphasis upon bold, simple and uncluttered visuals is not lost on set members who may have had to sit through tedious presentations peering at minuscule words and figures indiscriminately copied from the company report or other printed document.

Painstaking preparation is the key to presenting confidently. This extends to the very important, often threatening, area of dealing with questions. The workshop covers the skills of managing questions by techniques such as deflecting them or rephrasing them. More rewarding for the participant, the workshop goes on to demonstrate the ability of the set to prepare a list of most of the questions which are likely to come up. Having prepared this list, it is but a short step to preparing reasoned, positive answers. Confidence is bolstered.

But the essence of the presentation skills workshop is in the learning which comes from presenting and receiving feedback. During the two-day programme each set member should be able to give at least three presentations. Each presentation will be an improvement on the previous one because, after each presentation, the presenter will have had the benefit of objective appraisals from his or her fellow participants, from the video camera and from the tutor. Furthermore, the presenter will also have served as an appraiser, discussing the presentations of other set members, and will have learned from tutorial inputs as specific points arise.

The presentation skills workshop comes near the end of the action learning programme – week 26 on the schedule given in Figure 6.1. By this time the written report has been finalized, or is in the final stages of preparation. The set know *what* they want to say. Their concern is *how* to say it.

I normally design the workshop so that on the first day the set members arrive ready to give a ten-minute presentation on any subject of their choosing – usually a hobby. Over the years I have become surprisingly knowledgeable about the sex life of sea urchins, edible mushrooms of the Dordogne, tunic buttons of the British Army and other such esoterica.

Talking about their own interests allows the participants to concentrate on the delivery of the talk without having to worry too much about content. In a safe environment the set member can experiment with different methods of delivery, with different visual aids and with different ways of structuring the talk.

On the second day the emphasis is upon preparing for the final presentation, using all the techniques and knowledge gained from day one.

Presenting the learning summary

The presentation of the individual learning summaries normally follows on from the presentation of the project recommendations to the client and the panel. There should, however, be a gap separating the two sessions. Now that the more formal presentations are over a more relaxed feeling takes over. A tea or coffee break can effect the transition and allow some of the guests to leave unobtrusively. The presentation of personal experiences calls for a more intimate setting – maybe just the set, the client, the set adviser and two or three of those managers and tutors who have been deeply involved in the programme.

The one consistent aspect of the learning summaries is their diversity. It is as if all the lessons from the creative thinking tutorial were brought together to produce individualistic and original performances.

If any guidelines at all are to be given to the set members, it is that the presentation should be built around such headings as:

- *Learning styles* What can the set member tell us about his or her preferred learning styles? Were attempts made to strengthen the use of neglected learning styles? How will the set member take learning styles into account when planning future learning?
- *Feelings* How did the set member feel in given situations? How did he or she analyse feelings? Was there a pattern of cause and effect? What conclusions were reached for future reference?
- *Observations* What did the set member observe in terms of effective and ineffective behaviour? Did he or she find any particular model (e.g. behaviour analysis) useful? How did the set member modify his or her own behaviour in the light of these observations?
- *Using Q* How has the set member developed his or her skills in the Q of $L = P + Q$? What examples can he or she give outside the action learning programme?
- *Using P* What have been the most important elements of P? How will the set member make use of this P?
- *Personal planning* How does the set member propose to continue his or her self-development? What are the priorities? What help will be needed from the set member's manager, from peers and from others?

The list of learning skills identified by Mumford and cited on page 84 also provides a checklist to help the set member prepare the learning log summary. These and the headings above are thought starters. At this very personal level creativity soon takes over to produce learning summaries that are often imaginative and stimulating.

The length of time devoted to each presentation is usually governed by the size of the set, but a minimum of 5 minutes and a maximum of 15 seems about right. As in all presentations, the use of visual aids should be encouraged. Where large numbers are involved, say a set of 18 – three sub-sets of 6 – the presentations can be spread over two days. This has the advantage of avoiding presentation fatigue.

We have already said that a major benefit of action learning is that participants often have to talk to managers who are at a very senior level in the organization. For some junior and middle-level managers this contact is a revelation, demonstrating the different way in which top managers not only think but also behave. In presenting their learning summaries to the client's panel, and in answering the questions put to them, this exposure is continued. It is to be hoped that it also spills over into coaching and mentoring.

8 Implementing the recommendations

Much has been written on the theory of action learning, how to apply it and what results to expect. Very little, however, has been written on how to implement the recommendations arising from an action learning project.

One reason for this gap in the literature is that, by the time the action learning programme has reached the implementation phase, the action learning specialists such as the set adviser have withdrawn from the scene, leaving the internal organization to carry out the recommendations. It is the set adviser who generally has a vested interest in writing up the action learning experience, for academic or other reasons. We hope that, left to themselves, the set members will continue to keep their learning logs up to date, but this is a personal and private record. With few exceptions the implementation of the project recommendations goes ahead without a narrator.

A second reason for the lack of prescriptive guidelines is the diversity in the way in which recommendations are implemented. Even in the same organization action learning programmes are different in their impact and implications and require different approaches over different time spans.

We have emphasized that the setting up of an action learning programme should be proclaimed from every feasible vantage point and on every possible occasion. Action learning cannot take place in an organizational vacuum. The action learning set is made up of employees from different sectors and levels in the organization. They are going to move across functional boundaries, asking questions and collecting data. The existence of the set will be clearly visible.

In addition to this we are going to make action learning even more overt by publicizing the set's activities through bulletins, the house journal and even by videotape. The aim is to keep the whole organization up to date with how the set is progressing so that, when the recommendations are revealed, there will be no surprises.

Communicating action learning to the rest of the organization lasts the length of the programme – longer, in fact, if we take into account the communication that takes place before the start-up, and the communication that continues into the implementation phase. The set's presentation to the client and the panel is a powerful tool for introducing the shape of the changes to come. Put on to videotape it can be sent round the organization to be played informally wherever people gather, or formally during briefing groups and other meetings.

Overall the process of communicating the commitment to change may have been going on for as long as six to nine months, and sometimes longer.

Managing the implementation

Roger Plant[1] says that there are six activities which are key to successfully implementing change:

- Communicating 'like never before';
- Putting effort into getting support and commitment;
- Translating perceived threats into opportunities;
- Involving people at an early stage;

- Helping people confront change;
- Allowing for flexibility in the change process.

Plant stresses that putting concentrated effort into communicating that change is on its way, and what that change will (or might) involve, is an effective way of reducing the anxiety caused by uncertainty. Regular, consistent updates on the action learning set's activities stifle embryonic grapevine rumours. The very nature of action learning ensures *de facto* communication. What is needed in addition is a fully orchestrated communications campaign.

In discussing commitment to change, Plant refers to 'reward structures, employment policies and management practices' as the factors which induce long-term commitment to the organization. But he also points out that commitment can be generated by the presence of a problem which affects the short-term fortunes of the organization. The commitment of action learning set members comes partly from the recognition that they are indeed comrades in adversity. They are charged with finding a solution to a problem of real significance to the organization's future performance.

Implementing change smoothly in any organization depends on the extent to which those who are affected by the changes feel comfortable with them. The steady flow of information created by the action learning communication campaign does much to alleviate people's concerns about the need for change and how it will affect them personally. In addition, of course, each set member and the client becomes an emissary for change, able to discuss progress and implications with anyone who seeks information.

Some employees may have reason to feel threatened by impending changes resulting from the action learning recommendations. The organization will have to face up to this without prejudicing the outcome of the action learning programme. Those organizations (usually smaller ones) where change is seen as part of a continuing evolutionary process tend to manage change comfortably and successfully.

Plant's fourth point – getting people involved early in the

process – is covered in the natural development of an action learning programme. Crossing boundaries, seeking views and opinions, communicating vigorously, all involve people in the lead-up to change.

Helping people face change is about bringing the objectors, the resistance fighters and the backwoodsmen round to accepting change. Persuasion is preferable to coercion, and at the end of the day there may be some backwoodsmen still left skirmishing on the periphery. Often the last remaining objectors find themselves so isolated from their colleagues that, unable to beat them, they join them. In similar circumstances I have known managers, who initially refused to become involved in action learning programmes as set members, suffer so much from this isolation, the feeling of not being in the know, that they have later come forward with reasons why the set would benefit from having them as members.

Plant's last key activity for ensuring that change is managed well is that of leaving a degree of flexibility in the schedule for implementing change. Some organizations insist upon planning events to the *n*th degree, creating a real danger that adhering to the plan will take precedence over listening to feedback and making adjustments in order to get things right.

My experience has been that in action learning the implementation stage poses few people problems. From the very beginning action learning paves the way for the implementation of the proposals. The key to this successful implementation lies in the activities we have discussed: telling the rest of the organization why the action learning programme has been set up, what it is doing and how, working at gaining support and commitment throughout the organization, allaying people's fears, and planning flexibility into the implementation process. This last point is crucial. Having a highly structured plan for implementing the recommendations may lead to a delay in responding to changed conditions, in turn leading to frustration and even disillusionment. Today's employees are rational, intelligent people with a commitment to the organization. They resent being forced into changes which they neither want nor understand.

Fortunately, action learning belongs to what we have come to know as 'learning organizations', where attitudes and values ensure that that the preconditions for successfully introducing action learning already exist. And if the organization is not a 'learning' one before it introduces action learning, it very quickly becomes one.

Implementing the recommendations – some examples

Three examples of how the recommendations of action learning programmes were implemented will show the difficulty there is in any attempt to lay down hard and fast guidelines.

The first example describes the way in which a very small company implemented as they went along, leaving only a tidying-up operation to be completed after the final recommendations were made. The second example looks at a complex action learning programme carried out in a larger company, part of a large UK group. The third takes us back to the refinery action learning programme that we discussed in Chapter 1. The refinery is part of the UK operations of a multinational corporation.

Example 1
Our first example concerns Bentley Woolston, an eleven-strong graphic design company. The background, content and development of the programme, together with a review of the benefits that came out of it, appear in Chapter 10. This document was written by Richard Bentley, managing director of Bentley Woolston. It describes how action learning was brought in when the company realized that, unless they took immediate steps to redress their financial situation, they would very quickly go out of business.

This action learning programme is remarkable in that every

employee without exception was a set member. During the set meetings a receptionist from an agency came in and took over the switchboard. The set were able to work without interruption. Because of the need to get results quickly and implement them immediately, the programme was squeezed into a 17-week period that included the Christmas and New Year breaks – by action learning standards, a short programme.

Another noteworthy aspect of this programme was the way in which implementation happened along the way. It was a matter of driving the wedges in whenever the opportunity arose. Writing in May, less than two months after the end of the programme, Richard Bentley was able to say, 'Many ideas that emerged during the life of the programme were implemented immediately, the others since March.'

Foreseeing the pressure to implement ideas as quickly as possible, the set agreed, during the start-up workshop, that solutions which could be put into effect immediately should be – preferably overnight. They set up a system whereby individual set members were assigned responsibility for the implementation of specific recommendations. As the set meetings (many with tutorial inputs) progressed, more and more ideas arose for immediate implementation.

This set had one distinct advantage which again separated it from the 'normal' action learning set. The ultimate decision-makers (who were also the clients) were in the set. The speed of implementation was not hampered by long lines of communication.

The set adviser was heavily involved in the action learning programme from start to finish – and even beyond, as set meetings were convened after the official end of the programme. (These later set meetings looked into specific areas of the company's performance and were also used as an opportunity to initiate new members of staff into the ways of action learning.) The size of the company, the scale of the action learning project and the small number of personnel decreed that the set adviser was involved not only as guru of the action learning process but also as a resource to be used in getting the work done. A casual observer might well have mistaken the set adviser for a set member.

Example 2

The second example of implementing action learning project recommendations comes from Volvo Concessionaires Limited. The programme was concerned with three issues affecting the operation of the Parts Distribution Centre. Chapter 10 includes the record of an interview given by Peter Whitaker, the general manager responsible for the operation of the distribution centre. Having delegated the role of client upwards to his own manager at group headquarters, Peter Whitaker became a very active set member.

Of the three problems tackled by the action learning programme, one was pivotal, the driving issue: the need to redesign the pay system for the warehouse staff – and get it accepted. The other two issues arose from a real concern for the quality of life at work: the company wanted to introduce new methods of working which would give operators more control over, and satisfaction from, the work they performed, and it also wanted to bring in communication policies and practices that met the real (rather than the perceived) needs of all employees.

The set had no preconceptions of what the new working methods might be; their task was to create an environment in which the workforce would contribute their own ideas and have a decisive say in the final outcome. Similarly, they had no fixed ideas on the nature and shape of any new internal communication policies and practices. That would be a matter for joint exploration with all those in the communication network – in effect, all the employees.

The scheduling of this action learning programme was determined by the need to have the recommendations on the remuneration system prepared, and agreed in principle with the workforce, well in advance of the official wages round.

The set completed this aspect of the project in good time, and discussed their recommendations with the trade union representatives and officials. But, in Peter Whitaker's words, 'Not until negotiations were in full swing did both management and union sides become aware of a cardinal error. Although the management team [the set] had carried officials and representatives, the majority of the workforce were not in favour of the new arrangements. The hoped-for agreement failed to materialize.'

Chapter 10 describes how the set reacted to this setback, doubling their efforts to communicate directly with the workforce. In Roger Plant's terms they set about not only communicating as never before, but also working to allay people's fears, getting them as involved in the debate as possible and taking care not to be over-prescriptive or over-organized.

This Volvo Concessionaires' action learning programme was ambitious. It aimed to bring radical change into a sensitive area by abandoning a time-honoured remuneration system and putting in its place one which better served the needs of both staff and company. Coupled with this, it sought to speed up the move towards a performance culture by giving the workforce a large amount of discretion in the way in which they organized their work. In addition, it set out to test what employees and management wanted from the communication system, and then provide it. It succeeded on all counts.

To quote Peter Whitaker again: 'The results in terms of changes in attitude throughout this organization have more than paid off: we've now got a performance culture. . . . We're about a level of excellence that's light years ahead of similar businesses.'

The set adviser in this action learning programme was very deeply involved from the initial discussions through to the presentation of the recommendations to the client. He did not, however, become a set member in the sense of taking on a share of the workload. This allowed him to concentrate on oiling the wheels, guiding the process and safeguarding the learning. By the time the recommendations were presented the set had become self-sufficient and were able to carry the recommendations through to their final implementation, with the set adviser on tap but untapped. A fact of life for the consultant set adviser is that, if a job is well done, the set eventually becomes able to operate unaided.

Example 3

In the refinery example of an action learning programme all the set members (all foremen and supervisors from the maintenance department) were working on familiar tasks within a familiar setting (see Figure 1.1). The projects (there were three sub-sets each with its own project) were directly related to their everyday work. This made it relatively easy for many new ideas to be tested and implemented as the project developed.

Again, communicating played a significant role throughout the programme. The maintenance department saw itself as a scapegoat in the unremitting war against the vagaries of ill-intentioned plant and machinery. Here was an opportunity to demonstrate to the rest of the world the lengths they were going to in order to give a better service. They also recognized that, while solutions to 'local' problems could be implemented without reference to anyone outside the maintenance department, many recommendations would depend upon the good-will and co-operation of other departments, the production department in particular.

The impact of the recommendations would be felt most by the maintenance workforce. Working on the basis of involving as many people as possible as early as possible, the set used all the channels open to them to canvass opinions and ideas. In doing so they also allayed any fears that jobs would be changed out of all recognition, or existing skills would become redundant, giving way to new ones. Briefing groups, the house journal, bulletins, up-date talks, all were pressed into service.

The client was the departmental manager, which was convenient in that he was able to give the go-ahead to many solutions that were developed along the way. In other cases he negotiated on the set's behalf with his colleagues at departmental manager level. Most importantly, the client spent time keeping the middle managers in the department, the managers between the set members and himself, fully in touch with his own views on the action learning programme. This learning opportunity prepared the way for a later action learning programme involving middle managers from across the company.

With so much communicating going on from the start of the programme, there was nothing unexpected when the recommendations were finally announced. Although some drastic changes in manning levels, working methods and priority allocation systems were called for, the implementation went ahead with only the odd minor hiccup.

These three examples show the common theme of visibility through communicating. There is a window of opportunity which lasts from the moment the decision is taken to run an action learning programme, through to the final presentation to the client. Within this window of opportunity we communicate.

This communication is omnidirectional. It is proactive. It feeds information up, down and sideways. It seeks views and opinions from those who will be affected by the results of the action learning project, so that the hard facts of how people feel about change can be openly discussed and misgivings put to rest. Communicating makes certain that potential difficulties are recognized in time for something to be done about them. Come the recommendations, no one will be taken aback.

Every action learning programme starts life with one great advantage: the decision to introduce action learning has been made by a senior manager in the organization (the sponsor). This decision will usually have been reached after several protracted discussions with an action learning specialist. During these early discussions the decision-makers will have been made fully aware of the implications (see Chapter 3) of action learning for organizations in general and for their own organization in particular. The fact that these discussions have taken place at all means that the organization is a 'learning organization', or at least that the senior people want it to become one.

So support from the top, or from near it, is there at the

outset. The action learning programme is in itself a demonstration that those who run the organization really do want change *and are doing something about it.*

The client's role

Crucial to the communicating process and to the ease with which the implementation of the recommendations is carried through is the client. The client will have been working hard all the way through the programme to keep the set's efforts directed along paths that will lead to implementable solutions. Politically aware in the organization at large, he or she will have prepared the ground, anticipating difficulties and winning over doubters. Sometimes it will not have been possible or feasible to turn an influential objector into an ally, or even a neutral. At this juncture the client may have to advise the set to change its approach. The set's friend at court, the client will have been toiling behind the scenes to ensure that, when the recommendations are published, there will be no surprises.

The set adviser's role

During the run-up to the final presentation, the set adviser's contribution will have diminished in terms of the project work, although the learning and development side of the action learning equation, often too easily forgotten in the excitement of finalizing the project, will keep the set adviser fully occupied. Where the set adviser is an external consultant, the final presentation is often the point at which he or she bows out. Normally the set adviser remains on call over the ensuing few weeks or months, and may drop in to satisfy his or her curiosity about how things are developing. Working closely with the set members can lead to strong personal relationships which are not easily discarded.

In conclusion

Perhaps the implementation of the action learning recommendations can be best described as a non-event. There are no surprises. The programme flows from presentation into implementation.

Reference

1   Plant, R. (1987), *Managing Change and Making it Stick*, Aldershot: Gower.

Part 3
Action Learning Programmes

9 Alternative programme designs

The open set – the 'classical' approach to action learning

So far we have concentrated on the one-project-per-set, in-house approach to action learning. This is the model which is being used more and more in larger organizations because it is relatively easy to administer and control. There is, however, another approach – many refer to it as 'classical' action learning. This is the 'open' set model. Between the one-project set and the open set there are many hybrid forms.

A typical open set is one in which each set member brings his or her own problem to the table. Usually all the set members are from different organizations, although the set may consist of people from different units of the same organization, all working on different issues. Open sets may also house a mixture: say, two managers from one company, three from another, and seven from separate organizations. Within the set of twelve people, at least nine and possibly twelve problems will be being addressed simultaneously.

147

In an open set each set member uses the other members as consultants and advisers.

Open sets have several significant advantages.

- Organizations can put one manager into an action learning programme to gain experience of the process, develop the individual and address a key issue.
- Organizations can use open sets to bring together people from geographically widespread and diverse units. This offers benefits to large, complex organizations which need to develop managers across a wide range of functions and markets.
- Smaller organizations can invest in action learning on a local basis – for example, companies on a trading estate might share the cost of an action learning programme.

In many business schools and universities action learning has become a standard ingredient of management programmes, particularly those leading to the MBA and similar business degrees. Drawing students from many organizations, the open set is the norm, allowing people to follow their own projects, but with help from within the set, as well as from tutors and set advisers.

The extent to which action learning is used varies from institution to institution. The innovative MBA programme launched by International Management Centres in 1983 was the first of its kind to be designed and delivered entirely around action learning concepts. The philosophy behind the IMC concept was that, since their inception in the 1960s, the traditional business schools had spent their time taking in managers and turning out scholars of management. What was needed was a business school that took in good managers and turned out better managers. Action learning was the ideal vehicle.

The open set in action

Imagine a set of twelve people coming together two or three times a month for a set meeting. Each set member has brought his or her own problem to the meeting. As in the one-project set there will normally be a tutorial during the first part of the meeting. But after that the meeting takes on a different shape, with people breaking into sub-sets of, ideally, four.

During the remainder of the meeting each set member will 'present' his or her problem to the rest of the sub-set, explaining what work has been done since the last meeting, what the results were, what new difficulties have arisen and what further action he or she intends to take. The rest of the sub-set are consultants and advisers, playing devil's advocate, offering reasoned suggestions, and, above all, asking the apposite questions.

By the end of the allocated time the presenter makes a commitment as to what will be achieved before the next meeting. He or she returns to the organization well prepared to take the next step. The commitment to the set at large and to the sub-set in particular is a powerful driving force, compelling the set member to move the project forward in spite of recurring difficulties and frustrations.

Four seems to be the right number for the sub-set, bearing in mind that each set member must have adequate time to explain in detail to the others what has happened since the last meeting and what is intended for the future. Some sub-sets opt for a pattern which allows two set members to present for an hour each at alternate meetings. Thus each member has at least one hour every month or so in which to report to the working group and receive advice, guidance and support.

Three is also a viable number for sub-sets. It certainly allows greater time for the presentation and discussion of interim project reports, although at the expense of the variety of contributions from the rest of the sub-set.

The discussion that follows the presentation is objective and detailed. The comrades in adversity are bringing their diverse knowledge, skills and insights to focus upon the presenter's problems.

The open set start-up workshop

There are some significant differences between a start-up workshop suitable for an open set and the typical start-up workshop used for the one-project set described in detail in Chapter 5. This section deals with these differences.

In the open set, set members are called upon to be advisers and consultants to each other, working, as we have seen, in small sub-sets of three or four. If each set member is to fulfil adequately the role of adviser and consultant, he or she must quickly get to grips with the reality of:

- the organizations of the other set members – size, turnover, structure, products, processes, markets, culture, problems of the industry and of the company, and so forth;
- the jobs that the other set members do – key tasks, critical success factors, who they interface with, what the real challenges are, what constraints they have;
- the nature of the projects which each set member is going to undertake.

To achieve this, set members need to arrive at the start-up workshop armed with three documents:

- an organization profile
- a role profile
- a description of the problem to be addressed.

Based on these documents the participants will give presentations on their organizations, their part in them, and the projects they are about to start. The presentations are backed up by the distribution of the three supporting documents.

These presentations are given to the full set – in any event, the sub-sets, which are normally self-selecting, may not have formed. Furthermore, there is a danger that if the presentations are made in sub-sets the participants feel that the group that matters is the sub-set, not the set itself. Sub-sets can then become inward looking and miss out on the experience, insights and help available in the larger set. I have known one sub-set spend weeks on a particular issue, looking everywhere for advice, totally unaware that a set member in another sub-set held the key to their problem. Beware the 'them and us' syndrome.

The length of the presentations will depend upon the time available, but 40 minutes is about right, while 30 minutes is probably the minimum time in which to do an effective job. Rather than have one presentation after another it is better to spread them across the timetable. Two before lunch on the first day, one each side of the tea break, one in the evening, one first thing next morning, and so on.

An open set start-up workshop takes more time than its one-project counterpart. The participants will have put substantial effort into preparing material to bring to the workshop. In fact, action learning will have already begun, with individuals crossing boundaries and posing questions in order to get the information for the organization profile. In addition, the role profile will have caused the participants to re-evaluate the purpose of their jobs and the way in which they are done.

The client situation is more complicated than in the one-project set. Every set member should have a client, the person who owns the problem to be tackled by the project. But it is very unlikely that the clients will be at the start-up workshop. The set members themselves will have to take responsibility for agreeing a provisional definition of the problem and the project statement – provisional because these have still to be agreed between client and set member.

It is the sub-set who polish the problem definition and reach a project statement. This is the second step in the process whereby members of a sub-set reach a detailed understanding of each other's job and company.

'Jenny and I could swap jobs tomorrow,' said one burly production manager, 'and apart from the obvious nobody would know the difference.'

In the absence of clients, the set adviser and the project management tutor have a prominent part in helping the set members work on problem definition and project statements. The definitions and statements reached at the start-up work-

Time	Day 1	Day 2	Day 3
0900 – 1230	Welcome and introductions Background to the programme Introduction to action learning (I) Profiles and problems: Presentations 1 and 2	Presentations 7 and 8 Team effectiveness Presentations 9 and 10	Project design and management (II) *Problem definition *Project statement
1230 – 1315		Lunch	
1315 – 1730	Presentations 3 and 4 Introduction to action learning (II) Presentations 5 and 6	Presentations 11 and 12 Project design and management (I)	Project design and management (III) *Project scheduling *Resource allocation Logistics and domestic issues
1800 – 2000	Learning styles	Forming sub-sets	

* = Working in sub-sets

Figure 9.1 Typical three-day start-up workshop for an open set

152

shop will be checked and finally agreed with the clients when the members return to work.

In open sets there tends to be more frequent personal contact between the client and the set member. This is an ideal development situation if the client has sufficiently well developed coaching and mentoring skills.

Open sets and the set adviser

Before the action learning programme can get off the ground the set adviser has a lot of leg work to do.

He will have to visit each participating company not only to meet those who are immediately involved in the programme, but also to make sure that the projects being brought into the programme meet the criteria discussed in Chapter 4 – in particular, that they will result in significant change, that they are viable and within the scope of the set's ability, stretching them but not demoralizing them, and that they are likely to generate debate and give opportunities for creative approaches.

In addition, the set adviser will want to ascertain that both the client and the organization are committed to the success of the programme.

Briefing clients is time-consuming but of fundamental importance. The most effective way is to bring all the clients together for a half-day meeting, but often clients have to be briefed individually. One advantage here is that the set adviser can bring the client and the set member together and encourage them to talk through what each expects of the other.

Within each organization there is also the 'sponsor', the person who has been responsible for bringing action learning into the organization, usually the chief executive or the personnel and training manager. The sponsor will certainly want to be kept up to date by the set adviser on the progress of the programme and may at a later stage become involved as, for example, a tutor or a host for action research.

The set adviser's role in an open set action learning programme is very much that of a communicator, linking set members, tutors, clients and sponsors as well as fulfilling all the other duties of the one-project set adviser.

Logistics and the open set

Normally the only fixed points in an action learning programme are the date and venue of the start-up workshop.
During the start-up workshop the set take control and decide
where, when and how often they are going to meet.

The choice of venue for the set meetings is an issue that can
be debated at length – no big problem when all the organizations involved are close to each other. Solutions range from
one permanent meeting place (often a conference room at one
of the participating organizations) to a travelling circus, each
meeting being held in a different organization in rotation,
thereby giving the set exposure to each other's working
environment.

When the set comes from one area – for example, when all
their organizations are in the same town – the frequency and
length of set meetings are usually similar to those of our one-
project set. Three-hour meetings held two or three times a
month would be the norm.

When set members are based far apart a rotating venue
system is more usual. Again, on-site meetings are preferred to
hotels and conference centres. What does change is the pattern
of the meetings. In order to cut down on the travelling,
meetings tend to be longer and less frequent. One pattern is for
the set to meet for a complete day once every two or three
weeks.

Here, again, a caution. An underpinning principle of action
learning is that the social process, whereby set members
support each other, is paramount. Having too long a gap
between set meetings can have detrimental effects upon the
continuity of the programme and upon the commitment of the
participants.

Presentations to the client

As in one-project action learning programmes, the presentations to the client and the client's panel mark the end of the
formal programme. Only the implementation is left.

The presentation focuses upon those aspects of the written
recommendations that the set member wishes to amplify or

clarify. Following the presentation on the project results will be, in most cases, a summary by the set member of the learning that he or she has achieved during the course of the programme.

The question in the open set situation is, who should listen to the presentation? The client, certainly, but who else? The one-project set presents as a set within its own organization, so there is an immediate audience of set members and managers, all with a vested interest in this particular project.

What of the open set presenter? I have known many cases where set members have made excellent but solitary presentations to their organizations, without the moral, let alone physical, support of their fellow set members.

It would not be practical for all the clients of an open set to sit through all the project presentations, unless all the set members came from one organization, in which case there might be good reasons for bringing all clients and all set members together, despite the cost and inconvenience.

Many sets have found the answer in sub-sets: each set member invites his fellow sub-setters to be present when he makes his project presentation and his learning presentation to his client and the panel. In the audience are the two or three fellow sub-set members and the set adviser (friends and supporters), together with the client and other senior managers. Ample time can be allowed for questions and discussion. And by this time, all the sub-set members are intimately knowledgeable about the organization, its problems and the personalities involved.

After all the sweat and tears (and maybe even blood as well) that the set member has put into the project, this is a more fitting climax.

Joint venture action learning programmes

These are action learning programmes where two or more organizations join together to share the costs as well as the benefits of action learning. Where an organization recognizes the advantages of action learning as a problem-solving and developmental tool but does not have enough people to make an in-house programme viable, and does not want to send an employee off to join an open set, a joint venture is often the answer.

Typical of a joint venture approach is the case of a medium-sized chemical company which had successfully completed an in-company action learning programme involving 22 participants working in three sub-sets. The action learning programme had enabled them to claw back their share of a ferocious market.

Apart from being overjoyed at the bottom-line improvement, the chief executive had recognized changes in the behaviour of many of those who had taken part in the programme. He remarked in particular on their increased confidence, their wider outlook, their extensive in-depth understanding of the industry, and their ability to isolate factors which were critical to the company's performance.

Now, with retirements and expansion, the company was going to have to promote four middle managers to senior management positions within the next twelve to eighteen months. For each of them this would be their first appointment outside a purely functional role. The chief executive saw action learning as the vehicle for moving these managers from strictly departmental management to more general management.

The previous action learning programme had identified that the existing management information system was seriously flawed. There had never been a match between the business strategy and the information systems strategy. In fact, there had never been an IS 'strategy', although one was necessary to develop and maintain the business strategy. The computer systems had been brought in by information technologists. As in many organizations, the computer still belonged to the IT specialists and the accounts department, rather than to each and every manager.

An information systems strategy totally relevant to the needs of the business would significantly improve the company's ability to retain and improve upon its market position. Any action learning set addressing this issue would have to look at the company's business strategy first, and information strategies second. With proper direction they would never need to descend to bits, bytes and boxes. An ideal project for the four managers to tackle.

The chief executive considered running a second in-company action learning programme, but eventually had to dismiss the idea: he could prise the four managers in question away from their normal duties, and there were two other employees who would benefit from the action learning experience, but he could not justify the expense of running an action learning programme for only six people.

It was the personnel manager who suggested a joint venture. In the course of meeting regularly with other personnel and training specialists in the area, he had talked about action learning and the fact that, having had an excellent return on the investment in their first programme, they now wanted to run a second. However, the company had come up against the problem of numbers. Several personnel and training managers had pursued the matter further, and one had suggested getting several organizations together to run a programme between them.

The outcome was a joint venture programme. A retail organization came forward with five participants tackling the problem of integrating newly acquired businesses. A distribution organization provided a further five participants looking at the implications the opening of the channel tunnel would have upon its European operations.

I thus became the adviser to a set of 16 action learners who were to work in three 'company-based' sub-sets. Throughout the programme the sub-sets came together for all but the most esoteric tutorial inputs. During the start-up workshop it was stressed that the internal resources available came from having 16 people on the programme, and that the resources of three organizations were available to tap into for tutors and for action research. Although a person might be working in one sub-set, his or her skills and experience were available to every set.

To emphasize and take advantage of the large set situation, meetings were built into the programme devoted entirely to plenary up-dating sessions. Each sub-set would give a presentation to the others on the progress it had made, the problems it had met, and how it intended to proceed. The audience would then play devil's advocate, pose the apposite questions and test the thinking of the presenters, leaving them to reassess what they were going to do next.

In almost all respects the joint venture programme follows the pattern of the one-project action learning set. At the start-up workshop two or more clients are present or readily available (as in large in-company sets working in sub-sets on different problems). The main difference is in the wider learning opportunities created by the diverse backgrounds of the participants. The challenge is in harnessing this broad spectrum of skills, knowledge and experience.

The independent action learning set

An independent action learning set is one in which the set members are working on projects which are important to them at a personal level but are not supported by an employing organization. The set member is his own client.

It follows that independent sets are open sets, with the set members working on individual personal projects, using the other participants as consultants and helped by a set adviser and a range of external tutors.

Who then might join an independent action learning programme?

One example could be the chief executive who has a complex policy decision to make. By its very nature whatever he or she decides will impact upon the life and careers of employees at all levels within the organization. Boardroom colleagues will be affected, and some of them may have to accept early retirement. Further down the company it is possible that redundancies will have to be declared as branches are axed. Only one thing is certain: the chief executive cannot discuss the situation, float ideas and seek feedback within the organization.

Our chief executive is a decisive person, but wants his or her actions to be based on objective thinking which has been submitted to the scrutiny of an informed peer group. He or she needs to know that all the feasible options have been generated and evaluated. Other executives operating at a similar level must have found themselves in similar situations; our chief executive wants to tap into their experience.

Jill was 32 and unemployed. Leaving university with a good degree in mechanical engineering her first job had been with a multinational oil company, working at the company's UK refinery where, she complained, her male colleagues protected her from doing her job (at times a very dirty and physical one) to the full.

It took Jill four years to become disenchanted with her role as an engineer. She left and went to work for an agency which recruited clerical and administrative staff for jobs which required computer literacy and a nodding acquaintance with things technical. Two years later the firm collapsed.

Unable to recruit herself into the kind of job she wanted, Jill took the opportunity to become a freelance market researcher. This she thoroughly enjoyed, progressing from field researcher to work on survey design and then to sales. In 1990 this job also came to an end when her main client decided to appoint a permanent field research officer.

So Jill had a problem. At 32 she wanted a 'career'. What should that career be? After her halcyon days of freelance market research, self-employment remained an attractive proposition. But doing what? Should she become a licensee of some sort, or a franchise holder, or go on a course and become a consultant? Maybe multilevel marketing was the answer. Or could she in some way combine her engineering background with her recruiting and market research experience?

To add to the complication, should Jill go it alone, or was there any advantage in forming a partnership with a kindred spirit? Certainly, Jill did not know the way out of this complex situation. What she needed was the input of some comrades in adversity whose Q would help her see the way forward.

The first example, that of the chief executive faced with the reality of the loneliness of command, belongs to a type of action learning programme that is growing in application. Who can the chief executive share his thoughts and plans with in order to receive objective feedback? Who is going to submit the chief executive to the rigours of Q? Not the organization, but the independent action learning set.

Jill's case is different, and it illustrates an action learning application which has lain dormant since Reg Revans introduced action learning workshops for the unemployed in Wolverhampton in the 1960s. This use of independent action learning sets will develop rapidly in the coming years. As we move further into a work environment where planned, continuous careers become the exception we can look forward to a society where people have a series of discontinuous careers during their working life. Jill, at 32, is pondering what her next, her fourth, career should be. Note that we have said 'should be', not 'will be'. The ability to shape one's future is of the essence.

Jill joined an action learning programme when she was already between jobs. Many others use independent action learning programmes while they are employed in one career in order to prepare themselves for the next. Action learning programmes can meet in the evenings, at weekends, or at whatever time the set itself decides.

The self-facilitating set

The term 'set facilitator' is often used instead of 'set adviser': hence, a self-facilitating set is one in which all the set members share the responsibilities normally undertaken by the set adviser.

The self-facilitating set is a variant of the open set. Set

members work on their own individual projects, but without the services of an appointed set adviser.

The use of self-facilitating sets is confined to organizations where employees enjoy considerable personal autonomy and can schedule their workload so that they can free themselves from other duties to attend set meetings. There would appear to be ample scope for self-facilitating sets in such organizations as the Civil Service, research establishments, educational institutions, and other organizations where there is a high degree of concern for career and self-development among professional staff, coupled with the opportunity to form action learning sets which meet regularly over a period of several months.

It has been the educational institutions which have taken the lead in using self-facilitating action learning, with members of staff forming sets to address a variety of personal as well as work-related concerns.

McGill and Beaty[1] provide us with an excellent example of a self-facilitating set in action. Writing about one self-facilitated action learning programme undertaken by five members of staff at what is now the University of Brighton, they say:

From the outset there were three important ways in which this [self-facilitated] set differed from the traditional notion of an action learning set. First, action learning sets in organizations tend to have a 'client' outside the set to whom the set members are responsible for the progress of the task or problem. Although each of us was working on real problems directly pertinent to our job responsibilities, we did not have a client. We were our own clients using the set for our own purposes even though there would be a benefit to the organization for those of us concerned with pursuing tasks based on the organization. An example of this was taking a postgraduate management development programme from an interesting and rather novel idea through to successful validation and implementation.

Having no set adviser to chase, cajole and generally manage the action learning process, self-facilitating sets are entirely dependent upon the unflagging commitment of the set members.

This commitment is particularly critical when the set numbers only five or six members, the norm in self-facilitating sets.

McGill and Beaty[1] emphasize the fundamental importance of personal commitment:

When creating a new self-facilitated set the potential set members need commitment that is and remains voluntary. We do this by ensuring that the first meeting is a 'taster'. The first meeting works as a set but we are clear it is open to anyone to say that it is not what they anticipated and that they may choose not to come to subsequent meetings.

In an earlier work and in a similar vein, McGill et al.[2] remarked that:

For each person [in the self-facilitated set], commitment to the set and the way it worked was a priority. Being at the set was very important compared to the other activities associated with our work. This generated a feeling of protectiveness towards the time of the set. Something that required so much effort to protect and sustain could not fail to attain significance.

Current trends in the way that businesses are organized may lead to a greater use of self-facilitating sets as organizations continue the trend towards smaller and more autonomous units in which employees have increasing discretion in how they manage their time. The move towards 'one life, many careers' will heighten an awareness of the need for self-development. Action learning, adaptable and accessible, can satisfy that need.

With self-facilitating sets the dynamics of the action learning programme have changed from those of the traditional programme. Many of the structural elements are missing: they are no longer relevant. There is no formal start-up workshop – in a self-facilitating set, who would organize and run it? Who will tutor on it? Who will be the client? As many of the projects tackle personal issues (such as re-evaluating one's career plans, modifying behaviours, or pursuing a personal research project) the set member is inevitably his or her own client. An

Characteristic/element/component	One-project sets		Open sets			
	In house	Joint venture	In house	Joint venture	Independent	Self-facilitated
1 Company sponsor	✔	✔	✔	✔	✗	?
2 Client	✔	✔	✔	✔	✗	?
3 Set adviser	✔	✔	✔	✔	✔	✗
4 Formal start-up workshop	✔	✔	✔	✔	U	U
5 Tutors – internal and external	✔	✔	✔	✔	?	?
6 Workshops	✔	✔	✔	✔	U	U
7 Learning logs	✔	✔	✔	✔	✔	✔
8 Organization profiles presented	✗	?	✗	✔	✔	✔
9 Role profiles presented	U	?	✔	✔	✔	✔
10 Problem descriptions presented	✗	?	✔	✔	✔	✔
11 Formal report to client	✔	✔	✔	✔	✗	?
12 Final presentation to client and panel	✔	✔	✔	✔	✗	?
13 Presentation of learning log summary	✔	✔	✔	✔	U	✗

Key: ✔ = Yes   ? = Possible   U = Unlikely   ✗ = No

Figure 9.2 A comparison of the main characteristics of types of action learning programmes

acquaintance described her experience of a self-facilitating set to me:

It's a club, a coterie I go to every three weeks or so to tell the others – there's five of us altogether – about the work I've done on my project since our last meeting. Don't get me wrong. When I say club, I don't mean a place for casual social gossip. The reverse in fact. We work bloody hard while we're there.

Having to go and report, as it were, to the others, I make sure that I have something to tell them – I often feel that I am being driven forward by the momentum of the set. If I didn't accomplish what I said I would, I'd feel that I was letting them down.

When it's my turn to present my work what I'm looking for is constructive feedback. I will always collect some P – sometimes a lot of it – and that will rekindle my Q. Then I'm back on track again and find I've committed myself to doing the almost impossible before our next meeting.

Then it's my turn to critique what another set member has presented. On occasion I have supplied some P when the issue under discussion is related to accountancy and financial management – I once gave a talk to the set on getting finance for new business ventures. What does surprise me is how good I'm getting at asking the right questions, the ones that make people stop and think.

I am sure that I will finish my project. After that I don't know. I will have to leave the set, but it's comforting to know that if I have a new project I can rejoin the set . . . or start a fresh one.

I'm one of the ones who keep a learning log. I cannot see myself abandoning that. I realize now why some people keep diaries . . . but I think the logbook is much more useful than that. It forces me to reflect – and learn.

However, there must be a starting-point to action learning. Someone must introduce the concepts and framework of action learning into the organization. Although self-facilitation is the ultimate goal, a set adviser in the form of an external consultant will be needed to set the ball rolling. The first in-house action learning programme will be traditional, whether based on the open set model or the one-project model.

Passing on the skills of set advising to a shadow set adviser, together with an understanding of the action learning process, is part of the consultant's normal task. In the new situation each set member will be charged with gaining the skills and understanding that will enable him or her to spearhead the introduction of self-facilitating action learning.

Figure 9.2 summarizes the differences between the various types of action learning programme. The left hand column lists the main characteristics, components or elements which we have discussed as forming part of the action learning process.

The two main categories of action learning programmes – the one-project-per-set (sub-set) programme, and the open set programme – are shown in the remaining columns. These are subdivided into in-house, joint venture, independent and self-facilitated types of programme.

Reading across from item 2, for example, it will be seen that a client is necessary for all but the independent and the self-facilitated types of programme. For the independent set there is, by definition, no client. For the self-facilitated set there may or may not be a client. This will depend upon the nature of the individual project.

Similarly, reading across from item 8, we see that the presentation of organizational profiles is the norm for all but the in-house action learning programme, although they may be necessary for one-project joint venture sets which are made up of participants from different organizations.

The symbol '?' is used to suggest a 50:50 likelihood of a characteristic being present. The symbol 'U' indicates that its presence is unlikely, but not ruled out.

References

1   McGill, I. and Beaty, L. (1992), *Action Learning: A Practitioner's Guide*, London: Kogan Page.
2   McGill et al. (1990), 'Action Learning: a vehicle for personal and group experiential learning', in S. W. Weil and I. J. McGill (eds), *Making Sense of Experiential Learning*, Milton Keynes: Open University Press/SRHE.

10 Case studies

This chapter examines in detail two successful action learning programmes and looks briefly at three others which 'went wrong'. There are lessons to be learned from all of them.

The Bentley Woolston action learning programme

Bentley Woolston is an award-winning design and communications consultancy based in Milton Keynes.

In September 1989 the consultancy was in a poor financial situation and started an action learning programme to secure their long-term viability. At that time the company employed ten people.

Several months after the action learning programme had been completed, Richard Bentley, the managing director, submitted an entry for a National Training Award. The following is the text of that submission.

THE ORGANISATION

Bentley Woolston is a small mixed-discipline creative consultancy specialising in:

167

- Corporate marketing literature
- Visual identities
- Design-led direct marketing campaigns

[At the time] clients included ADT, Mercantile Group, BDO Binder Hamlyn, Lipton, Biffa, Museum Development Company and Cranfield School of Management. We work mainly in business-to-business communications.

THE TRAINING

The need for training was recognised in September 1989 when we were faced with poor financial results which threatened the continuing existence of our organisation. We knew that all our employees were skilled and competent at their individual jobs and that they were committed to the success of Bentley Woolston. We also had a sound and growing client base. Yet we were not financially viable. It was imperative that we got to grips with the problem.

Being a small company we called in outside help in the form of the Michael Reddy Organisation (MRO) and after several lengthy discussions with Scott Inglis, the Managing Partner of MRO, we agreed that we needed to do three things. The first was to harness the creativity and ideas within the organisation in order to solve our problems from within. The second was to get people working effectively as teams. The third was to help individuals grow and develop in preparation for wider jobs and new responsibilities.

The training vehicle we decided upon was Action Learning. Every person in the company was involved from partner to receptionist. From the beginning it was explicitly understood that the ideas and solutions generated by the Action Learning Project Groups would be implemented. Scott Inglis was to be the "Set Advisor" with MRO training consultants supplying specialist inputs whenever necessary.

The Action Learning programme got under way on 6th November 1989. It started with a two-day Start-Up Workshop. This Workshop was the only period of time spent off-site. The Workshop gave us the essentials for starting Action Learning, beginning with an understanding of the process of Action Learning (i.e. in the process of working as "comrades in adversity" pooling knowledge and resources to generate, evaluate and then implement solutions to problems, we, as a learning community, grow and develop). A glimpse of self-awareness followed when we completed the Belbin Self Perception Inventory before getting down to Project Design and Management. Here we became involved in defining and redefining our problem – or problems – and discussing and redefining until we were all agreed in our understanding of the issues. Force Field analysis took us a step further before we went into the process of restating the problem as two projects. We then moved to scheduling and resource allocation.

We came away from the Start-Up seething with ideas and eager to get on with the projects. Almost immediately came difficulty number one – there were not enough hours in the week to do our own jobs and complete our projects. Action Learning meetings were held from 3 o'clock to 6 o'clock and often beyond. In addition, both Project Teams managed to cram in quite a few lunch-time meetings. One Project Team looked at Quality issues, the other at Profitability levels. The essence of Action Learning is that participants drive the learning by calling for specialist inputs that they need in order to progress their work. The formal inputs we requested and received after Start-Up included:

Team Effectiveness
Client Care
Creative Thinking
Paper Management
Managing Change

The Team Effectiveness input was based on Margerison & McCann's Team Management Profiles and has resulted in the creation of four core teams around which the business is run – the Client Management Team, the Creative Solutions Team, the Efficient Resources Team and the Effective Delivery Team. Client Care is now a preoccupation based on understanding. Creative Paper Management has reduced – and made sense of – our filing systems. Managing Change has helped us to successfully implement the changes that came out of the Action Learning programme.

The Action Learning programme finished in March 1990. Many ideas that emerged during the life of the programme were implemented immediately, the others since March.

In terms of personal growth and development each one of us has a much wider and deeper knowledge of how our business works. We also have a heightened awareness of of our own strengths and weaknesses and the direction in which we want our careers to develop.

Action Learning came into Bentley Woolston to meet a given set of circumstances – what we didn't realise at the time was that we were acquiring, inter alia, a powerful Problem Solving Tool that we will continue to use.

THE BENEFITS

The three most significant benefits to emerge from this training initiative have been:

Improved profitability: Gross contribution on sales has risen from a year to date average of 32% in October 1989 to 43% in March 1990 and is still on an upward curve. At the same time overheads have been reduced significantly, enabling the consultancy to reduce the borrowings by 75% over a five month period. All this because the team now understands the ramifications of individual actions, particularly the recovery of chargeable time.

Improved Quality: This is an area where assessment of results is more subjective, but client response to the level of creativity and the quality of the finished product has been positive. There is a wider appreciation of quality standards throughout the team.

Improved teamwork: Our business depends heavily on teamwork to produce winning concepts and to meet fierce delivery deadlines. The improved teamwork has been highly noticeable and was, perhaps,the most significant contribution to survival during a period when high levels of productivity were required to achieve a sales-led recovery from a perilous financial situation.

We are a growing business with intensive client contact as a continuing demand on most staff. We see Action Learning contributing:

- to further improvements in profitability and quality
- to identifying individuals who have the capability to move into managerial roles
- to drawing out practical contributions from staff at all levels

We have fixed a further programme to integrate new members of staff.

In the absence of further financial incentives, we believe some kind of awards for training incentives by small business is critical. We invested a significant amount through loss of recoverable time and consultants' fees for this programme and yet have to identify any other scheme which encourages small firms to make this kind of commitment.

The Volvo Concessionaires Ltd action learning programme

Project VOCAL (Volvo Concessionaires action learning) was the name the action learning set at the Crick Distribution Centre gave to the programme which started in the autumn of 1987. VOCAL is exceptional in that the recommendations from the programme were not fully implemented until May 1989, some 19 months after the start-up.

Nevertheless, this was a successful and rewarding action learning initiative. According to Peter Whitaker, who was at the time general manager of the Distribution Centre, the programme gave the company distinct and lasting advantages over similar businesses.

VOCAL was an ambitious action learning programme. It became increasingly complex as action research opened up new avenues for exploration. As the central project dealt with sensitive issues and called for trade union involvement, the programme also had to cope with an external environment.

Early in 1990, almost a year after the recommendations had been fully implemented, Peter Whitaker gave an interview to Sarah Jones. By this time Peter Whitaker had accepted a board-level appointment as after-sales manager. The following is an article written by Sarah Jones immediately after the interview. Although Sarah Jones is an experienced action learning tutor, she had not taken part in VOCAL.

Volvo Concessionaires, Crick
Project VOCAL (Volvo Concessionaires Action Learning)
November 1987–May 1989

Volvo Concessionaires' Distribution Centre at Crick is currently in the throes of major, organisation-wide education/development activity. This activity is the outcome of an eighteen-month Senior Management Development programme, which had the ambitious aim of transforming the distribution centre into a service organisation.

According to Peter Whitaker, currently After-Sales Manager: "When we had to push through some radical changes for the organisation over the last few years, we decided to capitalise on the educational opportunities for the people in this organisation. That had to include everyone – from the management team to the distribution staff."

Volvo Concessionaires

Volvo employ about 75 physical distribution staff in the warehouse (hourly paid) and some 45 professional computer/sales staff, in addition to the small management team. Their UK parts distribution centre at Crick (part of Lex Service plc) currently services around 300 car dealerships in the UK and Ireland. The service aims primarily to support the dealer with parts and publications, so that the dealer can support the end customer – the buyer of the Volvo car.

Changes at Volvo – 1986/1987

Soon after Peter Whitaker's appointment as Parts Operations manager at the Crick site in late 1985, the management team was addressing the perennial question – "What business are we in?"

The answer was clearly that Crick was now definable in the service environment; 'not in the business of motor cars'. "People knew they were looking after our customer – the dealer. Our service to the dealers was reflected to the owner of the vehicle," reflects Whitaker. "The question remaining to be solved was how to turn "Fortress

Crick" (production-efficient, but customer-ineffective) into a service organisation, running to the highest quality and standards."

Two structural measures to achieve this aim were introduced early in 1986.

Firstly, the existing two-tier distribution system was rationalised. Regional parts centres were taken out altogether from the distribution chain, leaving the Crick base dealing directly with the dealerships.

Secondly, each dealer was now responsible for maintaining and ordering their own stock. To help the dealers with their stockholding, and help Crick service the dealers' routine – and urgent – requests for parts, Volvo introduced a totally new stock management programme into each dealership.

"We managed at the same time to put in a new office computer system, as well as changing one of our major suppliers", reports Whitaker. "It was an interesting time".

The following year, 1987, saw a further drive to improve service levels out of Crick.

Response to urgent demands for parts were improved in two ways. Firstly, dealers could now telephone for parts up until 2.00 pm and rely on delivery by 9.30 am the next day under the enhanced DUO (Daily Urgent Order) system. Second, very urgent "emergency" orders were despatched direct to the dealer by courier (under a system that came to be known as "flying bits").

Attention was also given to improving routine transactions with Crick's dealerships. The wait for a standard stock order was reduced from an average of 11.4 days days to a guaranteed five days.

And, of course, during this time the company was continuing to improve and apply the stock management programme.

Environmental factors, as well as internal restructuring, were starting to bring pressure to bear. A range of new models produced by Volvo in an expanding market brought an increase of one-third in the number of lines (different types of component) handled, year on year. More customers than ever before were returning to the dealerships with their service requirements, increasing the volume of parts, as well as the range of lines, needed by the dealerships.

What's the problem?

"Our problem," concedes Whitaker, "was that we asked the warehouse staff to deal with the growth in volume and lines. The result was that the warehouse wages – quite literally – took off."

In this relatively rural area, the company benefits from a loyal workforce who handle problems well and show considerable commitment to the business. Recruitment is limited because employee turnover was, and is, effectively zero.

The workforce enjoy an employment package and working conditions regarded as "very good". The unionised workforce in the warehouse (about 60 in 1987) have a positive, constructive relationship with the management at Crick.

By mid-1987, increases in volume and number of lines handled had pushed up bonus and overtime payments to the warehouse staff. This resulted in a 22% increase in wages in 1986 alone, well ahead of comparable market rates. Increased payments to warehouse staff highlighted a problem of "double indemnity". Staff had little or no incentive to adopt new technology, since inflated wage levels were linked to volume alone.

The increase in warehouse overtime reflected a long-term increase in volume, not simply a passing 'blip'. A more direct, linear relationship with the resources was clearly needed. The existing payment system (created 7 years before) reflected the volume handled, taking no account of quality and standard of service to the customer.

Recalling the time the problem surfaced, Whitaker reflects, "There was a wind of change moving through Crick. People realised things had to change; the interesting thing was how we were going to go about solving the problem."

With the new wage deal set up for renewal on 1 October 1987, the management team set out for "some fairly radical change" in April of the same year.

The pay system – and beyond

The management team set four clear objectives for the new payment system:

1. The new package had to reward quality, as well as volume, as well as to satisfy variable workloads.
2. Its design had to allow an element in the reward package that allowed the company to introduce new methods and/or systems to maintain the balance of reward and work effort.
3. Direct unit labour costs had to be reduced.
4. The new package had to at least hold the warehouse staff's gross wage at 1987 rates.

"This last element was a moral concern" Whitaker points out. "The warehouse wage had been driven up by our inability to manage growth".

Whilst others in the management team were keen to drive the pay package forward, Whitaker realised that this was a golden opportunity to tackle other issues around service excellence at the same time, including professionalism and customer service. He wanted to look at work group arrangements and the way that pay might be related to group behaviour. Communication had to be right as well.

"We realised that we should set objectives for the organisation and communication. We were a new team. My personal agenda was to seize a unique opportunity for devoting the time to ourselves for individual maturing through some sort of Senior Management Development programme for my team."

Having agreed on the objectives for the organisation and communication, the management team looked to a number of sources for help.

"We met with a number of consultants", says Whitaker. "They all had some sort of packaged solution which they saw as the answer to the problem. Nobody seemed to grasp the flavour of what we were after. They didn't seem to understand that we wanted to move employee relations forward. We wanted to get people involved in the process of change, to give them ownership of the solutions. None of the solutions that the consultants proposed seemed quite right.'

Enter Action Learning

Following up a lead given by a personal contact, Peter Whitaker asked the Michael Reddy Organisation to come to talk to the management team about Action Learning.

"We found the idea of Action Learning beguiling. We saw that it could give us a technique to solve our problems whilst developing us as individuals."

A number of factors were already operating in favour of this approach. The management team of five was already operating as learning "Set". The group had defined the extent of the "Project" in terms of the problem, and the time available for its solution. The Operations Director satisfied the three criteria for the "Client" in that he "owned" the problem, supported the Action Learning approach, and wanted a solution.

"Despite some scepticism amongst the team, we were attracted to the idea of "learning by doing" and saw the process as the only option which would meet both organisational and our own developmental objectives. Accordingly, we appointed the "Set Adviser" from the Michael Reddy Organisation to facilitate the learning process, and provide the expert resource we would need to succeed with the project."

Project Vocal

The set got under way with the project with initial start-up work. This involved taking a couple of weekends away with the group to study group dynamics and learning styles, open up relationship issues within the set, and learn techniques of project management and control.

One of the first stumbling blocks was the realisation that the group's initial objectives for the payment system, the organisation of work groups, and communications were "too flabby" and needed tightening up. It took some time for the group to tighten up these objectives. However, by November 1987 the project brief was approved, endorsed and, most importantly, supported by the Board. The Set were, in Whitaker's words, "suddenly expected to turn it all over."

There was, however, a price to pay for taking on a comprehensive project which attempted to provide a synthesis of these organisational objectives. The team had missed a crucial dealine (October 1987) for the round of wage negotiations. The group set a new deadline of October 1988 for a repeat round of wage talks, which would include the components the Set were currently working on. This time, the group had to "get it right."

To help push the project along, the group set up a project management workbench on an IBM PC, which helped them set milestones and loops. They also recruited two extra people in the group to feed logistics and analytical skills into the group. By this time, the Set realised how vulnerable they were. They felt that they had underestimated not only time, but people demands of the project.

How much time was the team investing at this stage? "An awful lot," admits Whitaker. "About half day a week, with several weekends and evenings thrown in. If I'd known how much work was going to go into the project, I suppose I might have hesitated. It was a fairly hectic time."

The project matures

One of the first steps taken by the Set was to run an attitude survey amongst the warehouse staff. They found feelings of frustrated talent; individuals felt that they had more to give than the company was currently asking of them. Importantly, the staff wanted their new payment scheme to recognise and reward group, rather than individual performance. Expressions of inadequate communication were balanced by feelings of high commitment, excitement, and positive signals for management about growth and development at Crick.

The Set addressed three prime areas of change and development; the payment scheme, work group organisation, and communications. After inviting three tutors in these areas to give talks to the team, Whitaker remarks that the quality of tutors contributing to the learning within an Action Learning Set is crucial – "a lot depends on who you get".

In order to get through the work within the time allocated, the Set split into three subgroups of two members each.

1. The Payment System

As part of the learning contract, the group charged with developing the payment system visited a number of companies, amongst them Metal Box, Renault, Marks & Spencer, and IBM. In all cases, bonus payments were found to relate back to quality, and as a result of these visits the group were able to make a number of recommendations to the Set.

Their stance was founded on a high basic, with no overtime for weekdays. Other elements included a quality bonus paid monthly, with dealer credits for missing, damaged or wronged parts; a "service platform" rota for Saturdays; commitment to automation; and individual performance counselling.

2. Organisation

As configured at the time of the project, the organisation of staff was seen to be fragmented. Dealer Support staff were responsible for taking orders, Purchasing bought the "bits", and distribution (warehouse staff) were responsible for delivery. No one person was responsible for overseeing the "whole picture".

The working group set itself the task of trying to remove as many stages as possible, in the belief that this would improve customer orientation (both internal and external).

A threefold reorganisation was recommended to the Set. First, that warehouse staff should handle complete orders, preferably for the same dealers; second, that dealer support staff should have specific dealers allocated to individual staff; and third, that the Purchasing and Systems Departments should set up internal "Help Desks".

3. Communication

The extended management team (16 individuals) spent the whole of a long weekend exploring, agreeing on, and talking about communications. It was decided to appoint a manager with special responsibility for communications (following the lead given by IBM). "The appointment of a manager in charge of communications didn't absolve the line manager from overall responsibility for communication – but in order to manage communications as a process, it was sensible to appoint someone at a very senior level".

One of the most strenuous tasks undertaken by the Communications group was the definition of the half-dozen key words describing the organisation's core values for internal communication. "This took an unbelievable amount of time".

The Set attempted to assess the risks involved in implementation in all three areas before moving into the "negotiations" starting at the beginning of October 1988.

Implementation of the Action Plan

By June 1988 the proposals in the three key areas were in a position to be endorsed by the Board.

In order to put the work group recommendations into practice, it was important to fix the new concept of internal customers into peoples' understanding. Ten "quality groups" were set up to cover aspects of service both inside and outside the organisation.

Issues such as the composition and remit of the "quality groups" were the subject of much discussion and debate both inside and outside the Set.

Whitaker sees the publicity surrounding the remit of the Set as fundamental to the success of its outcome. The Set ran a number of briefings; "I didn't feel we could keep it secret".

An internal marketing campaign under the slogan "You can make the difference" was launched to reinforce the standards implied by the core values the Set identified.

The company as a whole also undertook some communications skills training; although Whitaker comments, "This wasn't as consistent as we would have liked".

The debate on the payment system was initiated. Management and Union representatives were involved in full discussions, very positive and constructive up to reaching agreement. By October that year, however, major problems began to threaten the success of the negotiations.

Three-quarters of the Union representatives were off sick; the full-time assistant general secretary was promoted; and the team lost a key player in the Parts Distribution Manager.

Swift to mount a "holding operation", a new committee and management team regrouped to start the crucial negotiations in October.

Not until negotiations were in full swing did both management and union sides become aware of a cardinal error. Although the management team had carried officials and representatives, the majority of the workforce were not in favour of the new arrangements. The hoped-for agreement failed to materialise.

In spite of impatience from both sides, Whitaker firmly believed that a majority agreement to the proposals reached by the Set was essential to the success of their implementation. So, from late 1988 until Christmas, the management team braced itself to start again and gain the commitment of the majority of the workforce.

"This involved a lot of communications work. We had to talk to everyone about why we made the proposals we had, and how they were to be implemented. We had to be open about the risks".

As part of the communications work, the group set up "clinics" involving the management team over the period of a week. The realisation was dawning that management were not handing down "tablets of stone". Whitaker reports the feeling in the company at the time as "joint determination". Both sides reached agreement on the new pay package in Spring of 1989. The participative approach had paid off.

By 1 April 1989, the Set could justify the feeling that they had achieved the early stages of the attitude change they were seeking. First line managers were yet to be equipped with skills to manage this attitude change, as everyone had underestimated how much of an attitude change it was likely to be.

The benefits of the Action Learning approach – a retrospective

The action learning approach has brought many benefits. The team is far more aware of group dynamics, and relate to each other even though the team itself has changed. An honest appraisal of VOCAL "warts and all" has left Peter Whitaker in no doubt about the value of the process, although he has remained critical of the variable quality of some of the "expert input."

One of the most important aspects of the approach has been that the whole project has been "done by", not "done to". The involvement at every level of staff within the organisation has smoothed other transitions, including the introduction of a new computer system which was effected in November 1989.

The company is still continuing steadily down the road to developing distribution into autonomous work groups. Project teams are designing and making a series of "quiet revolutions" in terms of service initiatives.

As a result of the action learning programme at Crick, Volvo's car importation centre at Ipswich is currently planning an organisational intervention along the same lines.

Whitaker himself has now accepted promotion to After-Sales Manager – a Board level appointment. "The success of this project clearly helped," he comments. "From the outset, we made the 'people dimension' the focus of our activities. The results in terms of changes in attitude throughout this organisation have more than paid off; we've now got a performance culture at Crick.

"One can now see it in retrospect. We now have a complete management team who understand and are fully committed to the objectives that we have in running this site. We wanted to be far out in front of the field. We're about a level of excellence that's light years ahead of similar businesses."

Sarah Jones

Some that went wrong

People learn more from making mistakes than from getting things right first time round. Making a serious mistake can be a painful experience, and it certainly makes us reflect upon what went wrong so that we can do better next time.

The following examples illustrate action learning programmes which went wrong. None was a total loss. In each case both the organization and the set members benefited substantially, but in each case the set adviser had cause to reflect upon how the rewards could have been greater and the pain less.

Case 1

This is the case of a specialist recruitment agency – or 'body shop', as they frequently and disparagingly called themselves. The agency employed a headquarters staff of 32. All were young. The oldest, by seven years, was almost 40: most were in their twenties. The company was three years old and growing quickly. The problem it wanted to tackle was how to improve profitability by increasing market share and making internal administration more effective and less costly.

Given the initial enthusiasm and energy within the set of 15 (two sub-sets of 7 and 8), everything seemed to bode well for a rewarding and enjoyable action learning programme. As it was, four factors (two mechanistic and two organic) were to cause the programme to be aborted at an early stage. In ascending order of importance these factors were:

- condensing the start-up workshop into one day;
- the timing of the set meetings;
- the decision not to keep learning logs;
- the chief executive's expectations.

The one-day start-up workshop was held in a room in the main office – not an ideal venue, and open to interruption from the adjoining general office. The lack of time meant that most of the workshop was devoted to the task of defining the problem, translating the problem definition into a project statement, and discussing aspects of project design and management. The 'soft' areas such as the theory of action learning, learning styles and team effectiveness were glossed over. Numerate and results driven, the set was impatient to launch itself into the project proper. The lack of understanding of the process and of the personal issues was to bedevil the programme from the beginning.

Timing the fortnightly set meetings for eight-thirty in the morning seemed a good idea at the time. The intention was to carry on until eleven thirty or twelve noon. Unfortunately, no one foresaw the Cinderella effect: at midday the set were expected to stop the exciting, glamorous project work and revert to the mundane events of everyday office life. The outcome was unsettling and the midday switch to 'real' life detracted from the perceived relevance of the action learning programme.

The decision to do without learning logs made individual development an accidental (or at best incidental) part of the programme, rather than a central one. Set members could see what the organization were getting out of the programme, but they had no clear understanding of what was in it for them at a personal level.

The critical issue, however, was that of the chief executive's failure to accept the essential nature of action learning, and here the consultant-cum-set adviser must share the blame. During the initial discussions the set adviser had gone to great lengths to explain the relationship between P and Q, as well as the role of the set adviser as the 'owner' of the action learning process. It was made clear to the chief executive that the set adviser brought no special knowledge of the business – only an intelligent ignorance, the ability to pose, and get others to pose, the insightful questions that would lead to solutions.

In spite of this, throughout the life of the programme the chief executive looked for P, disappointed that the set adviser did not bring with him a deep knowledge of the industry. In the end the set adviser had to advise the chief executive to cancel the action learning programme and switch to a traditional consultancy approach in which 'experts' would give guidance for the company to follow.

Fortunately, by this stage many of the recommendations which had come out of the set meetings had been implemented. The action learning programme had already paid for itself.

Case 2

In this case the company employed over 200 people in the UK. The action learning programme was held in the company's headquarters and the 12 set members (two sub-sets of 6) were drawn from HQ-based managers and specialists. The problem they addressed was that of establishing a three-year marketing strategy which would take into account new entrants into the market-place and a spate of new products from existing competitors.

The failure of this action learning programme was the result of insufficient preliminary preparation. After two short meetings with the consultant set adviser, the chief executive decided to be both client and set member. The set adviser was not involved in the selection of the set members, and did not have an opportunity to talk individually to those selected before the programme began. The whole communication process was hurried through. The set adviser was concerned at the time that not enough care and consultation had gone into the initial stages of setting up the action learning programme, but in deference to the chief executive's wishes he went along with the decisions that had been taken.

Despite the set adviser's misgivings the start-up workshop went smoothly: the problem was defined, agreed and turned into a project statement. Resources were allocated and a schedule for the completion of the project drawn up, together with a list of dates for set meetings and workshops.

The real difficulties arose at the first set meeting. The set members were unable to work together effectively. Some felt that they had been coerced into joining the set. Others felt that they would have been far better employed 'getting on with their work'. Although these problems can occasionally surface in the early stages of the best-planned programme, in this case the feelings were so strong that it was decided to call a halt after the second set meeting. The action learning programme was put into abeyance.

Almost immediately the set adviser ran a team effectiveness workshop for an enlarged group of managers, on the basis that nothing further could be done until the management group could work together purposefully and cohesively. In achieving its objective the workshop highlighted the extent to which communication within the organization had dried up. The priority was to get communication flowing again as a preliminary to even thinking about long-term planning.

Eighteen months later there was talk about resuscitating the action learning programme, but by this time the culture of the organization and the nature of the market-place had radically changed. A new (and very successful) action learning programme was started from scratch.

Case 3

The third case was not a failure in terms of recommendations made and successfully implemented, but from the learning perspective it did not achieve what it might have done.

This is an example of an action learning programme being brought into one division of a large company following the success of an action learning initiative in a different division. Again the chief executive of the division was a set member, and again several set members had initial reservations about being there at all. And there was no learning log.

In contrast to the previous example the social relationships within the group were excellent, founded on years of working together. All seven set members were managers, and all had long service with the company. Three had spent their whole working life on the one site and for this reason feared that they might be 'exposed' in exploring the wider issues of the strategy-based project.

In many ways this action learning programme was very much the chief executive's property. He did most of the talking – and to compound the felony the others usually deferred to his point of view. Had it not been for the goodwill of long-established relationships, the programme might have foundered. As it was, in order to disturb the counterproductive comfortableness of the set meetings, the set adviser was forced to intervene frequently as a 'facilitator', just to ensure that opinions were challenged and ideas fully debated.

Not keeping a learning log, and allowing one set member too much say, limited the value of the programme as a means of personal development. That was the consensus of the set when I met them a year after the programme had finished. 'Had we to do it again,' said one set member, 'we would keep learning logs and insist upon some sort of presentation of the results at the end of the programme. Apart from anything else the discipline would be good for us.' Pressed to comment on the balance of contributions during set meetings, another set member concluded, 'One thing's for sure – we would certainly find a way of letting everyone have a fair crack of the whip when it came to voicing opinions.'

11 Action learning for the smaller organization

For the purpose of this chapter we can define a small organization as one in which there are no more than two levels between the chief executive and the first-line supervisor. It is unlikely to employ more than 200 people, and the chief executive may well have a financial stake in the company.

Small firms are growing in numbers and in sophistication. The splitting of larger organizations into small autonomous or semi-autonomous units through buy-outs and through decentralization has greatly increased the number of specialist small companies operating in the field of high technology. In addition, the advance of information technology and of complex technical aids has widened the horizons of the smaller organization. Many owners have invested in management training and education both for themselves and for their managers, and MBAs are increasingly being attracted into small companies, bringing with them an awareness of the importance of developing key people within the organization.

Peculiarities of the small organization

'I am convinced that the way of life of a small firm is so different from the culture of the medium-sized or large organization that the management manual has little to say that is of relevance, and even less that is acceptable, to the small business.' These are the words of the late David Sutton,[1] based on his experience of small companies, both managing them and introducing action learning into them.

While the organization remains truly small – perhaps with a founding father as chief executive and, say, two other managers – the systems through which the company is managed remain simple. Communication lines are short and direct. As growth sets in, the organization spreads both vertically and horizontally. To link together customers and suppliers and managers and specialists, more complex and unforgiving systems are brought in. To manage and control these now complex activities we have a level of managers working just below policy level.

These new managers come in over the heads of the managers who saw the company through its formative years. Formal systems and procedures now replace the *ad hoc* ones which used to work well in simpler days. There is a feeling of resentment and resignation in the air. Work is no longer meaningful, no longer fun.

It is at this point that the chief executive-cum-founder realizes that something must be done if the organization is to have a future. To quote David Sutton again:[2]

He [sic] is faced with two conflicting philosophies. Either he keeps face with the existing management team and strengthens it by supplementing it and developing the skills of the originals or he scraps the existing team by dismissals and replacements with newcomers. Each approach presents its own problems. He is between Scylla of the Peter Principle (each manager finding the level of his own incompetence and producing negative results) or the Charybdis of throwing out the baby of detailed knowledge and personal loyalty with the bath water of ineffectiveness. There is also the problem (which Sir Clive Sinclair never seemed to solve) of what to do with himself.

Action learning can and does help small companies through this kind of dilemma. Its effectiveness comes from its ability to focus people's attention on the reality of 'What can *we* do to make this company successful and a good place to work in?'

Isolation is something which all chief executives have to accept. In the large organization the size of the top management group means that the chief executive may have one or more colleagues with whom he or she can talk about all but the most sensitive issues. Some of these colleagues may be very close to the chief executive in terms of seniority, length of service and experience.

In a small company the situation is usually different. The chief executive is probably the only manager concerned with policy decisions, the only one in direct contact with the owners. With whom does he or she discuss the major sensitive issues facing the company? For many chief executives in small companies the answer lies in the open set action learning programme. Here the chief executive joins a small set of peers, each bringing his or her problem to the set, and using the other set members as advisers, consultants and confidants.

The open set and how it works is described in detail in Chapter 9.

A holistic approach to management training and development in the small business

Just to stand still in an ever changing environment, all organizations and individuals have to learn and adjust. Our world is continuously changing: new legislation, new products, new competitors, new constraints and new opportunities. What worked well yesterday is probably ineffective today and could be disastrous by tomorrow.

Small businesses have potentially one distinct advantage over their larger rivals. They are compact. Authority is centralized. Communication is quick. As a result the time taken to respond to change is (or should be) short.

In small companies the emphasis is upon being busy, getting on with the job. Outside the areas of production and marketing little if any attention is paid to searching out and investigating new approaches and ideas. The 'we've always done it this way, and its always worked for us' syndrome still lingers in many small businesses, but these businesses are becoming rarer, victims of their own myopia. Organizations which make a practice of using external consultants find that they acquire a mirror in which to see their own reflections, and the extent to which their own management practices might benefit from fresh ideas.

Teamwork in most small organizations is left to happen. Managers and others are all extremely busy, hard-working people, hemmed in by deadlines. They cannot really spare the time to attend meetings and get together with others to exchange information and plan. Yet it is because they have not learnt and developed the skills which are essential for effective teamwork that meetings take so long and accomplish so little.

So far we have argued that:

- Organizations, of whatever size, need to learn and adjust continuously merely in order to stand still. To progress, they must be able to learn effectively.
- Smallness bestows several advantages. One is the ability to respond quickly to change.
- Traditionally, small organizations look upon themselves as being able only to react to changes in the market-place. The reality is that small companies can be proactive.
- The development of teamworking skills has generally been neglected by small businesses.
- Except in areas such as R & D, production and marketing, small firms depend upon external consultants for the introduction of new ideas and practices.

When looking at action learning in relation to small businesses we should also go back to some of Reg Revans's early tenets.

The first of these is that there is a wide gap between the realities of life in a small (or large) company and the theories emanating from universities and business schools and some consultancies. Furthermore, it is a long time since most of today's chief executives were at university or business school. Enmeshed in the practicalities of running their businesses, these chief executives have lost any interest that they may once have had in theoretical issues.

However, these chief executives are the only people able to bring about learning and change in their organizations. It is therefore the role of the external consultant to supply and help implement a methodology which will enable him or her to do so.

Managers, especially those in small organizations, deal with concrete problems. They believe that they have learnt how to manage from their own personal experiences. They tend to recognize only the part played by their activist and pragmatist learning styles, discounting the reflector and theorist.

Managers respect managers. Managers will listen to other managers rather than to experts, however well qualified.

Managers, Revans found, habitually underestimate their subordinates and undervalue their views and opinions. But under certain conditions, however, this behaviour usually disappears. One set of conditions was that established in an action learning programme.

All the aspects we have discussed above are present in action learning. A concrete problem is solved, bringing a pay-off. The organization becomes a learning organization. Employees acquire new skills and new outlooks. The organization takes initiatives. Real teamwork gives the organization a real edge. Managers listen to subordinates – and even to experts.

The organizational growing pains

As we have seen, small firms need to adjust quickly as they grow. Their development tends to follow Greiner's[3] model of organizational growth very closely. Greiner identifies a pattern

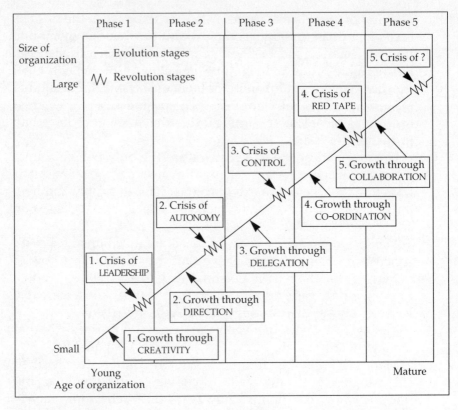

Figure 11.1   Greiner's five phases of growth

in which phases of growth and development are interrupted by outbursts of revolution, the crises that mark the end of one evolutionary phase and the start of another. Figure 11.1 illustrates Greiner's five phases of growth.

The first phase is that of creativity. The firm comes to life, inspired by an idea. For a while the important thing is to be creative, to do things differently, to steal marches on the competition. Inevitably the time comes for the first crisis – the leadership crisis, the issue of who has the final say: the innovators whose ideas created the company, or the producers and administrators who are concerned with the long-term commercial viability of the firm.

If the organization survives its first crisis, it will enter the second evolutionary phase, that of 'direction', or steady growth under professional management. This ends in the crisis of autonomy which challenges the directive management style. By now the business has become more complex and middle-level managers want more freedom of action and less imposed directives. By now the business may no longer be a small business.

If it survives this crisis of autonomy and lives through the ensuing phase of delegation it will sooner or later meet the crisis of control, caused by top managers feeling that they are losing control of what is now a diverse organization. They attempt to wrest back control, often by imposing centralization.

The co-ordination phase follows, to be brought to a halt by the red-tape crisis – the systems intended to co-ordinate all aspects of the company's activities have grown unwieldy, irksome and counterproductive.

After the red-tape crisis comes the collaboration period, with its emphasis upon teamwork, matrix management and customer service. Greiner predicts that the crisis to end this phase of evolution will be brought about by the 'psychological saturation' of employees who become emotionally and physically exhausted by too much interfacing with others and too little time for reflecting.

Greiner looks at the way in which an organization develops throughout its formative years. Obstacles to growth are generated by the natural process of evolution. Problems and issues arise as the organization passes through five distinct phases. Each phase is characterized by a distinctive manage-ment style. Each of these management styles eventually outlives its usefulness and becomes counterproductive, causing crisis. The crisis is overcome by a short period of revolution which addresses the issues and ushers in the next evolutionary phase. Greiner emphasizes that each phase is an effect of the previous phase and the cause of the ensuing one.

In small organizations this sequence of evolution and revolution, with periods of productive calm being shattered by regular but short periods of internal turmoil, can obscure the other very real problems and challenges which come from the external world.

We have studied examples of action learning helping the organization to surmount internal difficulties caused by the process of growth. Thankfully, action learning is also effective when the problems come from outside the company. Here, although similar in almost every way to action learning within larger organizations, there are a few marked differences in practice. These differences can be seen most clearly when we look at the role of the set adviser.

We have described Greiner's theory at some length because it highlights the root causes of many of the problems that beset smaller organizations. Large organizations also suffer crises, but as these organizations are by definition well along the evolutionary scale towards or into the collaboration phase, periodic pendulum swings have become a way of life rather than a threat to it. In small companies the immediacy of a crisis can cause great distress.

Action learning has a significant role to play in turning these problems into vehicles for growth and achievement.

One example of action learning being used to help a small business through its first crisis, the crisis of leadership, is the case of the small graphic design company cited in Chapter 4. The company had evolved along the lines described by Greiner. The design staff, headed by one partner, were extremely talented and innovative, producing exciting products that delighted clients and brought in new business. Theirs had been the vision and the impetus that had got the company off the ground.

But despite a full order book and a wealth of talent the company was in serious financial trouble. The administrators, the business people, recognized that the cost and consequences of unbridled design threatened the life of the company. The crisis had arrived. Action learning was called in.

In this action learning programme, which involved every one of the 12 employees, there were two sub-sets. One sub-set tackled the problems associated with design aspects (for example, Do we over-design? What *are* our design standards?), while the other addressed the profitability issue. It was the sub-set made up of design people who looked into systems and profitability. The administrative people were in the set investigating design standards.

The company came safely through the crisis. Chapter 10 contains an account of the action learning programme written by the client.

Another small company to use action learning to overcome a crisis was a supplier of specialist tools to the construction industry. In this case the crisis was that of autonomy. The chief executive, who reported directly to the owners, was extremely detail-oriented, a stickler for precise facts. Like many conscientious, detail-oriented managers, he found it difficult to delegate and thereby relinquish a degree of control.

The company had passed through the leadership crisis some years earlier and had entered the direction phase with gusto. Rules and procedures abounded. Any decision which did not fit neatly into the policy guidelines had to be sanctioned by the chief executive. The chief executive was overextended, the managers disgruntled, and the company slowing to a halt. Enter the crisis of autonomy.

The crisis came when the chief executive called a meeting to take his managers to task about worsening company performance. Suddenly the floodgates were open. The managers expressed their resentment and frustration at a system that prevented them from doing their jobs well. They had been forced to stand by and watch as the company first edged and then rushed towards disaster.

This outpouring of feelings heralded the arrival of the second crisis. To his great credit, the chief executive listened to his managers and then acted. On the basis that there was a major problem to solve and an immediate need for managers and other key people in the organization to grow and develop, he brought in action learning. The problem to be addressed was, 'What do *we* have to do to turn this company into a high-performance organization?'

Typical of action learning, in both these examples a problem that threatened the very existence of the organization was transformed into a vehicle for re-energizing the organization and its people.

A further example of an action learning programme in operation within a small organization comes from a publishing company going through the throes of expansion and re-organization. After a prolonged period in the evolutionary phase that Greiner calls creativity, the company was moving towards the direction phase. First, however, the leadership crisis had to be negotiated.

The founding fathers, the partners, had identified what their problems were and their own part in them. Symptomatic of the move from creativity to direction, they had decided on a strategy of removing themselves from the day-to-day operation of the company. They had also recognized the need to buy in expertise in what were now seen as critical areas for the firm's continuing growth, for example accounting and computing. In addition to this, the existing managers had to be developed so that new ideas and methods could be accepted and implemented.

There were some interesting features to this action learning programme. The whole management team below director level was involved, together with senior specialists. Previous management education and training within the set ranged from nil to an MBA. The programme was based on the open set model (see Chapter 9), with each set member bringing his or her own problem (related to his or her own job) and using the other set members as catalysts, consultants and advisers.

The open set model meant that every set member had his or her own client. In fact, all the clients were directors. Several directors were client to more than one project, and the client was not necessarily the set member's boss.

The set adviser first met the set members some time before the start-up workshop. There was what he later described as a 'compound of passive resistance, active hostility and fear'. The passive resistance merging into hostility came from the distrust of change: the fear came from the prospect of having at some point to stand up publicly and give a personal presentation to a panel who were not only directors but also distinguished academics.

The very experienced and capable set adviser behaved in every way as a model action learning set adviser should, responding to the requests of the set and making resources available to them as well as easing them through the action learning process. Otherwise he kept a low profile, leaving the set to get on with it – which they did, successfully.

Reflecting upon his performance after the action learning programme had finished, the set adviser expressed doubts as to whether he had, in fact, done the right thing. In terms of getting results – that is, solutions to problems – it would have been better, he thought, had he taken a more directive role. The dilemma, as he saw it, was one of priorities: which comes first, the solving of the problem, or the development of the people? In a small company, if the problem is not solved, there may be no people left to develop.

The set members were asked to comment on their experiences. An immediate result of the start-up workshop was that this assortment of people of different ages, qualifications, experience and accountabilities began to think and act as a team. They recognized very early on that they did not know very much about each other's jobs. The process of getting to know about each other's jobs, particularly the factors in the job which were critical to the success of the company, forced them to look objectively at strategic issues as well as more parochial ones.

The set said that they had picked up some invaluable insights into time management, interpersonal communications, influencing others, using the strengths of others, meeting deadlines, and making presentations, as well as the increased knowledge of the organization and the industry.

Like many action learners in small organizations (and in some large ones, too) there were personal sacrifices to be made:

Too good to be true? No. The time we spent complaining about lost evenings and weekends. The times we lost faith and enthusiasm, challenged the motives of the Board, argued and fell out, cursed the

Directors, slandered the Set Adviser, and swore we would never do it again. Yet, when it was over and we had made our presentations, we would have done.[4]

The set adviser in small organizations

In large organizations the set adviser's role is to get the action learning programme off the drawing-board and into the reality of the start-up workshop, and from there through to its final successful conclusion: the implementation of the set's recommendations. The rule is for the set adviser to stand apart from the deliberations and decisions of the set. He or she is there to service the needs of the set and to make sure that the learning and developmental aspects of action learning are not pre-empted in the rush to reach solutions.

Writing on action learning programmes in general, David Boddy[5] says:

Nominators, clients and participants each approach the programme with a variety of expectations about the programme as a whole and the part each will play in it. There are likely to be discrepancies in these expectations, and these need to be recognised and managed in the course of the programme. The [set] adviser's role in particular may need working out; the participants' expectations may well be that he is there 'to lead' or 'to teach' the group; neither of these would be compatible with action learning.

My own experience of working as a set adviser with small organizations is that the set adviser frequently has to step down from this pedestal. In small companies there is always a degree of urgency. Team building and 'training' (the acquisition of new skills and know-how) are seen as more important than individual development. Development does inevitably take place, and learning logs enhance the effectiveness of individual development. But the time constraints, the immediacy of the need to get implementable results in a relatively short time, and the lack of internal resources make the set clamour for all the help they can muster.

Thus, despite the academic pundits, in a small organization the set adviser may find himself or herself intimately involved in the affairs of the set: undertaking action research, leading debate, evaluating options, and behaving as a set member.

External (as opposed to internal) set advisers bring to the small company the advantages of objectivity, ignorance and good connections. Objectivity comes from not being bound up in the day-to-day machinations and personalities of the organization. The set adviser can steer the participants away from too much introspection. The value of intelligent ignorance is that it asks those searching questions which are only posed by those new to an organization or from outside it.

Having good connections is a hallmark of the good set adviser: the ability to get the right person to talk to a particular group on a certain aspect of a specific subject, or the ability to make the necessary introductions which enable the set to carry out action research in another organization. Who within the client organization is likely to know a successful sales manager in a similar industry who can discuss how to oust competition from your targeted market?

Large organizations frequently use external consultants to introduce action learning and at the same time train their own personnel so that they can resource future action learning programmes internally. The small organization has slightly different priorities. Without the personnel and specialization available to the bigger companies their objective is to be able to put future action learning programmes together whenever there are significant problems to be tackled.

The organization's experience of having completed at least one action learning programme, and their understanding of the action learning process, will enable them to move quickly. However, it is unlikely that they will be able, or even want, to do without some external assistance. The set adviser who led the company through their previous action learning programme is asked back.

On this occasion the set adviser has much less to do. The phases preceding the start-up workshop will probably be well under way by the time he or she becomes involved: the problem to be confronted, the set members and the client will probably be known. The start-up workshop itself may be a condensed affair, and some inputs may be delivered by participants who were members of the last set. The set advising role that the organization requires is that of masterminding the action learning process and making sure that individual development does not get lost in the headlong rush for solutions.

In action learning people learn from each other. The second and subsequent action learning sets will almost certainly have participants who are new to action learning. Invariably, the experienced set members take over the education of the newcomers, again reducing dependence upon the set adviser.

With a nucleus of experienced action learners within the organization, and a friendly set adviser on call, the organization is ready to address internally many of the problems that would otherwise have been farmed out to consultants – marketing consultants, production consultants, personnel consultants . . . the list goes on.

External specialist help may still be needed, but on the company's terms and within the framework of action learning. When P is needed the request is: 'Come and talk to our team about such-and-such an aspect of this subject. We shall brief you fully beforehand. And after you've spoken and answered questions, we want you to spend the rest of the time working with our project team.'

The involvement, commitment and development that comes from using action learning to address issues is a far cry from the detachment of handing the problem over to consultants so that they can come back and tell you what to do.

Set advisers' fees – a footnote

Many freelance trainers and training consultants ask for fees based on high daily rates, whether they are talking to large organizations or to small companies. Where the client is a large organization the fees can often be justified in terms of the organization's expectations and the standard of presentation and support service required.

Small companies need a different approach. Small businesses want to invest in a long-term relationship with the consultant who is going to work with them over a period of years and who will come to know them and their problems intimately. The consultant's contribution to the company's profitability should increase as the relationship develops.

Most independent trainers have a similar interest. Long-term relationships means less time spent having to market services to one organization after another on a jobbing basis, never really getting beneath the corporate skin – an expensive way of doing business.

Small companies and independent trainers might well consider an arrangement based on a retainer. Most external set advisers are also well qualified in the wider field of training and development, and an arrangement which covered all facets of training and development, including action learning, would have benefits for both company and consultant.

This would also allow the consultant to look at a range of possible training and development solutions in relation to a problem, rather than just the action learning approach. Action learning is powerful when relevant, but there is always the danger that the unscrupulous may pervert it to a methodology in search of an application.

Being a set adviser in a small organization can be exciting and demanding (though maybe not the most financially rewarding for the consultant set adviser). The shorter time span between the implementation of the set's results and the impact upon the bottom line, the sensation of working with a 'complete' business, the personal relationships which are developed and the immersion in the company's culture and fortunes all contribute to a feeling of belonging and contributing – a feeling that many consultants say they find lacking when working with large organizations.

References

1   Sutton, D., (1984), 'Management Development in the Small Business', *Journal of European Industrial Training*, vol. 8, no. 3, Bradford: MCB–University Press.
2   Sutton, D., (1987), 'The problems of developing managers in the small firm', *The Action Learning Resource*, Bradford: MCB–University Press.
3   Greiner, L. E., (1972), 'Evolution and revolution as organizations grow', *Harvard Business Review*, July–August.
4   Sutton, D., (1987), 'The problems of developing managers in the small firm'.
5   Boddy, D., (1981), 'Putting Action Learning into Action', *Journal of European Industrial Training*, vol. 5, no. 5, MCB–University Press.

Part 4
Appendices

Appendix 1
Checklists for action learning

Checklist 1: Is the organization ready for action learning?

This organization:	Nearly always	Usually	Infrequently	Hardly ever
actively encourages employees to put forward ideas				
shows flexibility in dealing with difficulties				
gives all employees adequate training for the job				
encourages 'group think', e.g. brainstorming				
initiates change, rather than merely responds to it				
gives people the recognition due to them				
cultivates harmony between working groups				
uses a participative management style				

	Nearly always	Usually	Infrequently	Hardly ever
works hard at communicating to all employees				
helps people to develop their potential				
promotes from within whenever possible				
fulfils its commitments to employees				
TOTALS				

Introducing action learning will in itself reinforce the behaviours listed above, or move the organization emphatically towards them. However, if the total number of ticks in columns 3 and 4 is significantly greater than the total in columns 1 and 2, then some preparatory work is probably needed before action learning is introduced.

Checklist 2: Pre-start-up activities

Selecting the set members

Have you considered:	Yes	No
those with specialized knowledge of the problem?		
those who will be affected by ensuing changes?		
those with specific short-term development needs?		
those with long-term development needs?		
those who can contribute to the 'balance' of the set?		

Selecting the client

Is the client:

	Yes	No

easily accessible (e.g. on site)?

easily approachable by set members?

able to fulfil roles of coach and mentor?

able to influence the set's thinking without being directive?

a good listener?

fully committed to action learning?

Has the client authority to implement the set's recommendations?

If not, does the client have direct access to the person with that authority?

Selecting the set adviser

	Yes	No

Is the set adviser sufficiently experienced in action learning?

Is the set adviser well connected in terms of tutors, contacts, etc.?

Is the set adviser able to influence top management?

Has the set adviser a good understanding of general management?

Is the set adviser capable of taking a low-profile role?

Does the set adviser have adequate facilitating skills?

Will he or she be inclined to over-facilitate?

	Yes	No

Can the set adviser be directive if the need
arises?

Is the set adviser capable of being a counsellor
to set members?

Selecting the project

	Yes	No

Will the project provide adequate learning and
development opportunities?

Will it bring about significant change?

Will it stretch the set members without being
threatening?

Is it complex enough to generate a range of
possible solutions for evaluation?

Is it politically feasible?

Is the client fully committed to a successful
outcome?

Selecting the tutors

	Yes	No

Does the tutor have action learning
experience?

Is his or her style appropriate for your set?

Is the tutor prepared to become involved in
hands-on project work?

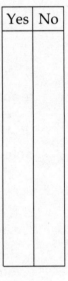

	Yes	No
Is he or she willing to conform to the set's brief?		
Will the tutor present P in a manner that generates Q?		

Checklist 3: Preparing for the start-up workshop

	Yes	No
Have the dates been agreed and the venue decided?		
Has everybody involved been told?		
Has the set adviser briefed:		
opening speaker?		
client?		
set members?		
tutors?		
training/conference centre staff?		
Have arrangements been made with the venue for:		
layout of main meeting room?		
arrangement of any break-out rooms?		
use of visual aid and other equipment?		
supply of tea and coffee?		
meals?		
accommodation for participants, tutors, etc.?		
interception of telephone calls?		

Checklist 4: Communicating the action learning programme

	Yes	No

Have we taken every opportunity to communicate fully?

a) before start-up, by telling employees:

that action learning is being introduced?

why action learning is being introduced?

who will be involved as participants?

when the start-up will take place?

who the client will be?

what the exxpected benefits to the organization will be?

b) after the start-up workshop:

the definition of the problem to be addressed?

the project statement that was agreed?

the initial schedule that was agreed?

where, when and how often the set is to meet?

c) during the life of the programme:

how the programme is progressing?

any major difficulties the set has met?

any significant milestones reached?

d) after the presentation of the recommendations:

summary of key points?

	Yes	No

schedule for implementation?

benefits gained from the programme?

how employees will be affected by the
changes?

e) throughout the implementation phase:

Have we made full use of the available means
of communicating:

notice-boards and bulletins?

house journals?

briefing groups?

question and answer sessions?

video recordings of question and answer
sessions?

video recordings of the presentation to the
client?

Have we told *all* the organization – not just
our corner of it?

Appendix 2
Typical action learning projects

The 30 examples of action learning projects listed below have all been completed within the last ten years. Many were undertaken on a one-project-per-set (or sub-set) basis. Others were completed by set members working within open sets. Some of the one-project sets were joint ventures involving two or more organizations.

The titles follow as closely as possible the 'official' wording of each project, although the names of the organizations have been omitted. In addition, in some cases the wording has been altered by replacing occupational jargon with more meaningful vocabulary.

The projects are taken from both the public and private sector and include:

Central government	Banking and finance
Education	Service industries
Chemicals	Local government
Leisure	Manufacturing
Civil engineering	Transport
Information technology	Health services

1. Developing income-generating units within an educational institution.
2. Strategies for growth in a property development company.
3. Reducing employee turnover in a civil engineering department.

213

4. Relocating the packaging plant of a manufacturing company.
5. Improving airside services (unloading) at an international airport.
6. Introduction of a computerized information system within an international food, drink and tobacco company.
7. Establishing corporate venturing strategies in a chemical company.
8. Gaining a competitive edge in telephone manufacturing.
9. Reducing manufacturing cost in an engineering company.
10. Changing the role of a public sector training organization.
11. Introducing succession planning to add value to HRM.
12. Matching performance to customer expectations.
13. Competitive business strategies after deregulation.
14. Profit improvement through quality.
15. Demand and capacity management for yarn business.
16. Expansion of private patient facilities to ensure revenue.
17. Development of accounting and financial reporting systems.
18. Implementing a computerized radiology information system.
19. Establishing new businesses in Third World countries.
20. Computerized approach to improving fleet management.
21. Post-merger role of a newly acquired research department.
22. Reducing work in progress and throughput time.
23. Survival and growth in a small company.
24. Replacing remuneration systems in a unionized workplace.
25. Developing strategies for operating from a European base.
26. Improving fleet management.
27. A policy for privatization in a local authority.
28. New product marketing strategy.
29. Implementing total quality management.
30. Gearing remuneration to the performance of sales people.

Appendix 3
The team effectiveness workshop (two days)

During the start-up workshop the set used Belbin's Self-Perception Inventory (see Chapter 4) to identify and probe their individual preferred team roles. In the period between the start-up workshop and the team effectiveness workshop, the set members will have had time to get to know each other not only as comrades in adversity but also as co-workers in a project team. Set members will have used the insights gained into how teams work: they will have become conscious of their own behaviour within the set, and of the behaviour of their fellow set members. Now, after some three or so set meetings, the group will be ready for a more detailed look at the work preferences within the set, and how the mix of individual preferences could affect the set's performance.

The set is faced with the task of producing implementable solutions to significant and complex problems. To work cohesively and successfully the set must shape itself into a balanced team. A set of six 'action men' would be unthinkable as would a set of six philosophers. Getting the right mix of attributes and work preferences is all-important.

In order to achieve the right mix and operate effectively, the set needs to understand and apply the principles that make an otherwise ordinary team into one which consistently performs excellently.

There is another side to the equation: no set member can

achieve a high personal performance without an understanding of his or her own work preferences, as part of an ERSI.* The important thing is for each set member to recognize and build upon the strengths and opportunities offered by his or her work preferences. Areas which the set member sees as not a preference (and therefore a 'weakness') should, of course, be noted (possibly for future remedial action), guarded against and offset. But personal development and growth nevertheless comes from recognizing our strengths and then building upon them.

Of the several team effectiveness models which can form the basis of the team effectiveness workshop, I prefer the one developed by Charles Margerison and Dick McCann.[1] This is centred on a personal profile derived by computer from a 60-item Team Management Index (TMI). The TMI measures individual work preferences in four key areas:

- how people relate to others
- how people collect and use information
- how people make decisions
- how people organize themselves and their work.

Running to some 4000 words, each profile discusses the preferences of the individual in relation to the four factors shown above. Each set member is also 'mapped' on to a Team Management Wheel for ease of discussion and for clearer understanding of the issues involved.

Content of the team effectiveness workshop

Pre-workshop
The set members fill in the Team Management Index (TMI). This is processed by computer to produce an individual Team Management Profile (TMP) for each participant. The TMPs become the core material for the workshop.

---

* ERSI: Extraordinarily realistic self-image (see Chapter 2).

Session 1

Characteristics of a high-performing team – what makes some teams achieve excellent results consistently?

This session builds upon the personal experiences of the set members to produce a set of ground rules for high performance. These ground rules form a reference point throughout the workshop.

Session 2

Individual Work Preferences – Session 2 identifies nine areas of work activity:

- advising: collecting and disseminating information
- innovating: creating and trying out new ideas
- promoting: selling ideas and getting support
- developing: assessing new ideas and methods, and modifying them where necessary
- organizing: setting up systems for work to be done
- producing: operating the systems and producing the goods
- inspecting: checking that the systems are correctly used
- maintaining: ensuring standards and values are upheld

Set members check out perceptions of their performance and behaviour with each other. Because of the shared experiences of the start-up workshop and ensuing set meetings, this is a supportive, non-threatening experience.

Session 3

This is the main part of the theory input. Session 3 explains the extent to which the personal work preferences mentioned above affect the contribution the individual set member makes to the work of the set.

Set members are led through an examination of where they perceive they operate from on each of the four factors. At this stage the TMP produced from the TMI has not yet been issued to the set members. The perceptions noted in this session will later be compared with the TMI results and form a basis for further discussion in Session 5.

Session 4
The Team Management Wheel – the model of the Team Management Wheel is introduced together with an examination of the strengths and weaknesses associated with each of the eight basic profiles:

- Reporter–Adviser
- Creator–Innovator
- Explorer–Promoter
- Assessor–Developer
- Thruster–Organizer
- Concluder–Producer
- Controller–Inspector
- Upholder–Maintainer.

The TMI will show where each set member lies within the Team Management Wheel.

Session 5
TMPs and implications for teamwork. Set members are given their profile printouts. The profile shows the set member's main preferred role together with his or her supporting roles.

The set members read and annotate their printouts individually before checking with the rest of the set and discussing the implications. It can take an hour or more for this initial reading and discussion, but it is important that this session is not skimped.

Session 6
Reinforcement of teamwork concepts – the balanced team. Session 6 starts with a few practical exercises to reinforce the concepts already discussed. It then introduces the concept of Team Balance and examines the make-up of the set in terms of team balance. The set is then in a position to look at its collective strengths and weaknesses and plan accordingly.

Session 7

Linking skills – applying them within the set. Set members work there way through a specially prepared Linking Skills Workbook.

Finally, the set examines how well the various concepts of Linking, Balanced Teams and High-Performing Teams apply within the set. Using the insights gained from the TMPs about the work preferences within the set, they agree on action to enhance the set's performance.

Reference

1 Margerison, C. and McCann, R. (1985), *How to Lead a Winning Team*, Bradford: MCB–University Press.

Appendix 4
Useful organizations

International Foundation for Action Learning (IFAL)
46 Carlton Road
London   SW14 7RG
Telephone & Fax: 081–878 7358

IFAL aims to identify and encourage a network of enthusiasts to support and develop the use of action learning worldwide. Membership, open to both individuals and organizations, provides opportunities to meet and learn from others actively engaged in action learning.

Association for Management Education and Development
  (AMED)
21 Catherine Street
London   WC2B 5JS
Telephone: 071–497 3264

AMED is an association of individuals who have a professional interest in the development of people at work. AMED aims to promote best practice in the fields of individual and organization development, to provide a forum for the exploration of new ideas, and to offer opportunities for members' professional development.

International Management Centres (IMC)
Marriotts
13 Castle Street
Buckingham   MK18 1BP
Telephone: 0280 817222
Fax: 0280 813297

IMC is the post-experience business school which pioneered the use of action learning leading to MBA and similar management qualifications. It is a valuable point of contact for organizations and company-sponsored managers seeking to gain qualifications while working on action learning projects.

Scott Inglis
Training Consultant
2 Park Cottages, Church Lane
Lathbury, Newport Pagnell
Bucks   MK16 8LA
Telephone & Fax: 0908 613692

The author of this book, Scott Inglis, specializes in running action learning programmes for client organizations.

Further reading

With few exceptions the literature on action learning falls into one of two categories. The first category consists of the material written by Reg Revans. This sets out the fundamental philosophies of action learning, tracing their development and describing the early action learning initiatives. Two books are recommended below for those who want to delve into the background and original flavour of action learning.

The second category is made up of a myriad of articles which have appeared in learned journals over the last two decades. These articles were (and still are) written by academics and practitioners for academics and practitioners. Fortunately, the most helpful of these articles have been gathered together in edited collections. Two of these collections – *Insights into Action Learning* and *Action Learning in Practice* – are cited below.

Action Learning – a Practitioner's Guide, although written by academics, is intended for a wider readership and marks the emergence of a third category aimed at the 'general' reader.

I have also included publications which cover topics closely related to action learning. While set advisers and tutors will have the necessary in-depth knowledge and skills in these areas, the general readers will find dipping into these books both illuminating and rewarding.

Background reading

Revans, R. W. (1984), *Sequence of Managerial Learning*, Bradford: MCB–University Press.

Revans, R. W. (1982), *Origins and Growth of Action Learning*, Bromley: Chartwell Bratt.

Action learning theory and practice

McGill, I. and Beaty, L. (1992), *Action Learning – a Practitioner's Guide*, London: Kogan Page.

Mumford, A. (ed.) (1984) *Insights into Action Learning*, Bradford: MCB–University Press.

Pedler, M. (ed.) (1991), *Action Learning in Practice* (2nd edn), Aldershot: Gower.

Weinstein, K. (To be published in 1995), *The Experience of Action Learning – A Journey in Discovery Development*, London: HarperCollins.

Related topics

Belbin, R. M. (1984), *Management Teams – Why They Succeed or Fail*, London: Heinemann.

Bennett, R. and Oliver, J. (1988), *How to Get the Best from Action Research – A Guidebook*, Bradford: MCB–University Press.

Garratt, R. (1987) *The Learning Organization*, Aldershot: Gower.

Honey, P. and Mumford, A. (1986), *Manual of Learning Styles*, Maidenhead: P. Honey.

Margerison, C. and McCann, D. (1985), *How to Lead a Winning Team*, Bradford: MCB–University Press.

Mumford, A. (1980), *Making Experience Pay*, Maidenhead: McGraw-Hill.

Mumford, A. (1993), *How Managers can Develop Managers*, Aldershot: Gower.

Index

Action learning
  ambiguity, role of, 27
  as act of faith, 34
  as agent for change, 10, 24–5
  as organization development, 26,
    30
  associates, use of, 65
  challenge, 57
  commitment to, 11, 37–40, 41,
    135
  competitive edge, 103
  contract, 7, 68, 126
  coping with uncertainty, 24
  core questions, 9, 34, 105
  crossing boundaries, 6, 58, 134,
    151
  definition, 3
  in small organizations, 187–201
  learner driven, 6, 8, 29, 66
  learning opportunities, 26, 45–60,
    8, 82
  limitations of, 51
  misconceptions about, 3–4, 17
  misuse of, 81
  model of, 98–100
  openness and trust, 25
  opens up debate, 59
  personal time, 50
  political aspects, 8, 13,33
  project based, 6, 10–12
  publicising, 134
  reasons for introducing, 56
  social process, 9, 67, 154
  terminology, 12
  theory base, 7–10

  time taken for programme, 7, 92
  visibility of, 6, 7, 10, 40, 134
Action Learning Trust, 21
  see also International Action
    Learning Trust (IFAL)
Action Research
  as change agent, 104
  as means of exposure, 58
  complexity, 106
  core questions, 105
  cost consideration, 106
  examples, 107–109
  general, 105–113
  methods, 106
  purpose of, 105
  role of set advisor, 106
  sequence of, 105
  survey by interview, 109–111
  survey by questionnaire, 107–9
  visits, 111–13
Activist, 15–16, 69, 81, 121, 191
Anxiety, 135
Assessor Developer, 218

Belbin, M. *see* Self Perception
    Inventory
Benefits, 23–4, 32–36
  examples of, 170–71, 180–181
  from learning log, 69–70, 81
  from management development,
    24–30
  from self-reliance, 32–3, 199–200
  from tutorials, 29
  long term, 81
Brainstorming, 29, 115
Business games, 19,

225

Dealing with Difference

Teresa Williams and Adrian Green

It's the first morning of the training course you've rashly agreed to run. You look round the assembled group and what do you see? Men and women, under-20s and over-60s, white faces, black faces, suits, jeans. Is there anything you can do – anything you should have already done – to make your training effective for people with perhaps widely different ways of regarding the world?

Yes, a great deal, according to Teresa Williams and Adrian Green. In this pioneering book they examine the effects of culture on the learning process and put forward a number of ideas and activities designed to help trainers take account of cultural values in the planning and delivery of their training. After examining both organizational and national cultures they look in detail at how diversity can affect every aspect of the learning event, from the initial announcement, through pre-course work and administration, to running the event itself and the subsequent debriefing and review.

The authors' approach will enable trainers to:
- design learning that acknowledges each participant's culture
- reduce prejudice and stereotyping
- run learning events that do not force participants to compromise their own culture
- achieve a better return on investment by working with the prevailing culture rather than inadvertently opposing it.

Contents

Part 1: Culture and Training • Introduction • What is culture? • The trainer's role • Part 2: Learners from Different Cultural Groups • Organizational culture • National differences • Part 3: Culture and the Learning Event • Advertising literature • Application forms • Joining instructions • Briefings and briefing notes • Pre-course work • Pre-course questionnaires • Icebreakers • The main event • Breaking the rules • Debriefing, feedback and review • Part 4: The Way Forward • Cultural dimension • The transfer of learning • Into action • Appendix: the implications of culture – an action checklist • Sources and resources • Index.

1994   216 pages   0 566 07425 7

Gower

Empowering People at Work

Nancy Foy

This is a book written, says the author, "for the benefit of practical managers coping with real people in real organizations". Part I shows how the elements of empowerment work together: performance focus, teams, leadership and face-to-face communication. Part II explains how to manage the process of empowerment, even in a climate of "downsizing" and "delayering". It includes chapters on networking, listening, running effective team meetings, giving feedback, training and using employee surveys. Part III contains case studies of IBM and British Telecom and examines the way they have developed employee communication to help achieve corporate objectives.

The final section comprises a review of communication channels that can be used to enhance the empowerment process, an extensive set of survey questions to be selected on a "pick and mix" basis and an annotated guide to further reading.

Empowerment is probably the most important concept in the world of management today, and Nancy Foy's new book will go a long way towards helping managers to "make it happen".

Contents

1994   288 pages   0 566 07436 2

Gower

Evaluating Management Development, Training and Education

Second Edition

Mark Easterby-Smith

This ambitious book offers a comprehensive guide to evaluation as applied to management development. It deals in detail with the technical aspects of evaluation, but its main value probably lies in its treatment of more subtle and possibly more important questions such as the politics of using evaluations, the range of purposes to which they may be put, and the effect of different contexts on evaluation practice.

The new edition reflects the many changes that have taken place in the world of management since the original text was compiled, in particular the Management Charter Initiative and the move towards competence-based training. The text has been updated throughout, and many new examples and case studies have been added, including a number from Europe and North America.

For anyone concerned with management development, whether as teacher, trainer or consultant, Dr Easterby-Smith's text will be indispensable.

Contents

Part I: Aims and Purposes • Introduction • Purposes and styles of evaluation • Part II: Design and Methods • A framework for evaluation • Data collection media • Data collection methods • Interpreting and using evaluations • Part III: Applications: Evaluating Methods, Courses and Policies • Evaluating methods • Evaluating courses, programmes and systems • Evaluating policies • Moving on? • Index.

1993   216 pages   0 566 07307 2

Gower

A Handbook for Training Strategy

Martyn Sloman

The traditional approach to training in the organization is no longer effective. That is the central theme of Martyn Sloman's challenging book. A new model is required that will reflect the complexity of organizational life, changes in the HR function and the need to involve line management. This Handbook introduces such a model and describes the practical implications not only for human resource professionals and training managers but also for line managers.

Martyn Sloman writes as an experienced training manager and his book is concerned above all with implementation. Thus his text is supported by numerous questionnaires, survey instruments and specimen documents. It also contains the findings of an illuminating survey of best training practice carried out among UK National Training Award winners.

The book is destined to make a significant impact on the current debate about how to improve organizational performance. With its thought-provoking argument and practical guidance it will be welcomed by everyone with an interest in the business of training and development.

Contents

Introduction • Part I: A New Role for Training • Introduction to Part I • The context • Models for training • Appendix to Part I: A survey of best training practice • Part II: The New Processes • Introduction to Part II • Training and the organization • Training and the individual • Performance appraisal • Design and delivery • Effective information systems • Part III: Managing the Training Function • Introduction to Part III • The role of the training function • The task of the trainer • Appendices: The UK training environment • National trends • Government policy • Competency-based qualifications • Index.

1994   240 pages   0 566 07393 5

Gower

How Managers Can Develop Managers

Alan Mumford

Managers are constantly being told that they are responsible for developing other managers. This challenging book explains why and how this should be done.

Moving beyond the familiar territory of appraisal, coaching and courses, Professor Mumford examines ways of using day-to-day contact to develop managers. The emphasis is on learning from experience - from the job itself, from problems and opportunities, from bosses, mentors and colleagues.

Among the topics covered are:
- recognizing learning opportunities
- understanding the learning process
- what being helped involves
- the skills required to develop others
- the idea of reciprocity ("I help you, you help me")

Throughout the text there are exercises designed to connect the reader's own experience to the author's ideas. The result is a powerful and innovative work from one of Europe's foremost writers on management development.

Contents

1993   240 pages   0 566 07403 6

Gower

Managing Upwards

Jonathan Coates

Would you like your staff to take more decisions on their own initiative? Would you in turn like to exercise more influence on your own boss? And on your peers in other departments?

In this refreshing new book Dr Coates challenges the assumption that management is a downward process. He analyses what happens within the organization and sets out ways in which managers can encourage involvement and creativity.

Using "real life" examples and case studies from three continents he shows how the necessary structures and attitudes can be developed – as well as the dangers of ignoring the problem. Among the issues he tackles are lateral relationships, the role of performance appraisal and the personal skills needed to make the new approach effective.

This is a book for all managers who want to develop the full potential of their teams – and themselves. Could it be that *Managing Upwards* is actually the surest road to organizational success?

Contents

1994   112 pages   0 566 07485 0

Gower

A Manual for Change

Terry Wilson

Change is now the only constant, as the cliché has it, and organizations who fail to master change are likely to find themselves undone by it.

In this unique manual, Terry Wilson provides the tools for planning and implementing a systematic organizational change programme. The first section enables the user to determine the scope and scale of the programme. Next, a change profile is completed based on twelve key factors. Finally, each of the factors is reviewed in the context of the user's own organization. Questionnaires and exercises are provided throughout and any manager working through these will have not only a clear understanding of the change process but also specific plans ready to put into action.

Derived from the author's experience of working with organizations at every level and in a wide range of industries, the manual will be invaluable to directors, managers, consultants and professional trainers battling to help their organizations survive and flourish in an increasingly turbulent environment.

Contents

Using this manual • Change programme focus: The scale of change • Change process profile: The twelve factors • Factor one Perspectives: Maintaining the overall view • Factor two The change champion: Leading the change • Factor three The nature of change: Identifying the change affecting us • Factor four Unified management vision: Importance of management agreement • Factor five Change of organizational philosophy: Modernizing the organization • Factor six Change phases: Four phases of change • Factor seven The 10/90 rule: Vision and real change • Factor eight Transitional management: Management role and style • Factor nine Teamwork: Importance of teams • Factor ten Changing behaviour: Identifying the critical factors • Factor eleven Expertise and resources: Assessing requirements • Factor twelve Dangers and pitfalls: Planning to avoid difficulties.

1994   191 pages   0 566 07460 5

Gower

Outdoor Development for Managers
Second Edition

John Bank

The use of outdoor activity on management development programmes is growing steadily. When John Bank's book was first published in 1985, it was the first full-length study of the subject. For this new edition he has revised the text throughout to take account of recent developments. It explains the underlying concepts, examines the relevance of outdoor training to management performance and reviews the range of programmes available.

The author draws extensively on the experience of people directly involved, both as trainers and as participants, and in ten fascinating case studies he shows how a variety of organizations use outdoor development in pursuit of their objectives. The book now includes details of eighty-eight outdoor development organizations and the complete text of the guide to best practice produced by the Development Training Users Trust.

Contents

1994   192 pages   0 566 07395 1

Gower

Participative Training Skills

John Rodwell

It is generally accepted that, for developing skills, participative methods are the best. Here at last is a practical guide to maximizing their effectiveness.

Drawing on his extensive experience as a trainer, John Rodwell explores the whole range of participative activities from the trainer's point of view. The first part of his book looks at the principles and the "core skills" involved. It shows how trainee participation corresponds to the processes of adult learning and goes on to describe each specific skill, including the relevant psychological models. The second part devotes a chapter to each method, explaining:

- what it is
- when and why it is used
- how to apply the core skills in relation to the method
- how to deal with potential problems.

A "skills checklist" summarizes the guidelines presented in the chapter. The book ends with a comprehensive matrix showing which method is most suitable for meeting which objectives.

For anyone concerned with skill development *Participative Training Skills* represents an invaluable handbook.

Contents

Acknowledgements • Introduction • Part I Principles • The nature of participative training • Planning and preparation • Briefing • Monitoring • Reviewing • Feedback • Working with people • Part II Methods • Question and answer • Buzz group exercises • Syndicate exercises • Case studies • Demonstration role plays • Skills practice role plays • Projects • Discussions • Game simulations • Fishbowl exercises and behavioural games • Experiential exercises • Support activities • Appendix: Choosing a method • Index.

1994   200 pages   0 566 07444 3

Gower

Teambuilding Strategy

Mike Woodcock and Dave Francis

There is no doubt that working through teams can be an effective way to accomplish tasks in an organization. As Woodcock and Francis point out, though, it is by no means the only one. Managers concerned with human resource strategy cannot afford to assume that teamwork will always be the best option. A number of questions need to be asked before any decision is made, such as:

- what should be the focus of our organization development interventions?
- should we undertake teambuilding initiatives?
- how extensive should the teambuilding initiative be?
- what resources will we need to support our teambuilding initiative?

This book provides a framework within which these questions may be addressed. It presents a structured approach to analysing the key issues, including a series of questionnaires and activities designed to guide the reader through the key strategic decisions that must be taken by any organization contemplating a teambuilding programme. The authors, two of the best known specialists in the field, examine the benefits and dangers of teambuilding as an organization development strategy and offer detailed guidance on further information and resources.

This is the second and considerably reworked edition of *Organisation Development Through Teambuilding*, first published in 1982.

Contents
Preface • Introduction • Part I Is Poor Teamwork a Significant Organizational Problem? • Organizational Effectiveness Areas • The Organization Development Priorities Survey • Part II Does the Organization Require a Team Approach? • Key Teams and their Effectiveness • The Teambuilding Priorities Assessment • Part III Is the Team Ready for Teambuilding? • Teambuilding Readiness • The Teambuilding Readiness Survey • Part IV Does the Organization Have Competent Teambuilding Resources? • The Competencies of Team Development Facilitators • The Teambuilder's Competence Audit • Part V Do We Need a Teambuilding Consultant? • The Teambuilding Consultant • The Team Development Consultant Audit • Part VI Building Effective Teams • The Eleven Building Blocks of Team Effectiveness • Practical Teambuilding – A Guide to Resources • Index.

1994   160 pages   0 566 07496 6

Gower

Training Needs Analysis
A Resource for Identifying Training Needs, Selecting Training Strategies, and Developing Training Plans

Sharon Bartram and Brenda Gibson

This unique manual is designed as a practical tool for trainers. It contains 22 instruments and documents for gathering and processing information about training and development issues within your organization. This frees you from the time-consuming business of formulating methods for generating information and allows you to concentrate instead on the all-important task of making contacts and building relationships.

Part I of the manual examines the process of identifying and analysing training needs. It reviews the different types of information the instruments will generate and provides guidance on deciding how training needs can best be met. This part concludes with ideas for presenting training plans and making your findings and proposals acceptable to others.

Part II contains the instruments themselves. They cover organizational development, organizational climate, managing resources and job skills. Each section begins with an introduction which defines the area covered, describes the instruments, and identifies the target groups. It also provides a checklist of the preparations you will need to make. The instruments themselves represent a wide range of methods, including card sorts, questionnaires, profiles and grids.

Effective training requires a serious investment in time and finance. This manual will help you to ensure that the investment your organization makes will achieve the desired results.

1994   200 pages   0 566 07561 X Hardback   0 566 07437 0 Looseleaf

Gower